THE DIGITAL STORY

Binary Code as a Cultural Text

Grant Kien

ISBN-13: 978-1540740069
ISBN-10: 1540740064

Irrepressible Press Publishing
Oakland, CA

DEDICATION

This text is dedicated to all of my outstanding graduate students, past and present. This is where my academic journey began. May yours be as rewarding as mine has been.

CONTENTS

APPENDICES

ACKNOWLEDGMENTS & NOTES

This manuscript has been modified for formatting, corrections and clarity from the original, a thesis submitted to the Faculty of Graduate Studies in partial fulfillment of the requirements for the degree of Master of Arts.

The Joint Graduate Program in Communication and Culture
York University and Ryerson University
Toronto, Ontario

Accepted September 20, 2002

Examining Committee:
John O'Neill, Supervisor; Fred Fletcher, Chair;
Jennifer Burwell; Barbara Crow; Brian Singer;
George Comninel

00000 INTRODUCTION

In the 17th century, a young man named Gottfried Wilhelm Leibniz became fascinated with the ancient Greek idea that all things in the universe could be expressed through a language of mathematical symbols. He thought he could invent mathematical operations using such symbols to describe the entire truth about life and the universe we live in. By simply substituting concepts for the symbols in the equations, even the most difficult of life's problems would become a matter of calculation. Leibniz later thought that a machine could be invented to perform these calculations, thereby making our lives that much easier — he thought with such a machine it would no longer be necessary for us to fret over difficult concepts and decisions. In spite of his efforts and the work of many others contributing along the way, it wasn't until the 19th century that a system of what came to be known as calculus was invented that satisfied much of the criteria Leibniz and his cohort, Isaac Newton, had laid out. In the 20th century, a second component of Leibniz's vision was realized with the invention of the electronic digital computer. Since the attainment of these technological aspects of his vision, Western society has been working to convert as much information as possible into the binary digital code with which the computer works, contributing to the fulfillment of his three-century old idea.

There is a great deal of work being produced about the emerging 'digital world' that we in Western society are said to inhabit, indicating a broad concern regarding the types of changes accompanying the technology. Analysis of social systems, interpersonal relations, political economy, and numerous other phenomena are incorporating the digital (r)evolution into the mix. The emphasis on the digitization of society in social and cultural research indicates the importance of this change in technological orientation. In spite of fleeting recognition of digital code as the primary medium of digitization, many social scientists and cultural theorists are hesitant to deal with the issue of the code itself, often leaving such discussions at the level of a very basic technical explanation. However, understanding the basic assumptions and cultural values embedded in digital code, as well as the way it functions on a technical level, is necessary in order to develop an understanding of its farther-reaching social implications.

Though as computer users we don't directly see it, digital code is actually a language system that expresses thoughts and concepts, and as such forms descriptive texts as Leibniz envisioned. In other words, digital code expresses decisions for its users according to the tasks put it to. Like any other, digital text can be analyzed and thereby understood in terms of history, social relations, processes, and knowledge in general. Like any other artifact, digital text can reveal the cultural intersections and implications inherent in its production, transmission and consumption. James Carey wrote, "To study communication is to examine the actual social process wherein significant symbolic forms are created, apprehended, and used" (1989: 30). Work in digital social studies has left a deficit of understanding about how the code is actually created and how it symbolizes, focussing more on how it is used. The emphasis on effects studies may unintentionally lend credibility to the idea of an assumed technological determinist evolutionary process beyond our human control. As the proliferation of digital technology exponentially increases our human capacities for speed in movement of both matter and information, understanding the aspects productive of digital code is a necessary undertaking if we are to maintain a conceptual grasp of the world we —aided by our machines— are creating. 'Us' and 'we' in this thesis refer to all of us who use or are affected by computers and digital code in any way, shape or form.

This thesis contributes to a fuller understanding of the nature of digital code as a cultural text, focusing on its philosophical and material origins. In the process, some of the epistemological effects and societal implications this format of information processing and storage was intended to bring about are exposed. More specifically, the social processes it mainly focuses on are those of human thought as it is represented by binary code. It also emphasizes that the purpose of computers is to mediate digital code, and elaborates some effects on cultural production for the contemporary user of computer technology. The end result is a different understanding of the character of our relationship with our technology than is often encountered in social theory.

Much writing on the effects of digital media tends to hyperbole due to what may be a misunderstanding of the nature of the code behind such media. Much of the discourse being produced on the subject of technology is prone to rhetorical overstatement, stemming from both a lack of understanding about the limitations of the technology, and even from willful misinformation (Baldwin *et al*, 1996: 2). The extreme responses of utopian and dystopian prophesizing may be attributable to William Ogburn's theory of "cultural lag", which "suggests that the effects of a technology will not be apparent to social actors for some time after it is introduced to a society" (Fisher & Wright, 2001: 2). Of course, none of this stops anyone from speculating anyway, and this thesis is no exception. However, this project contributes to a description of digital code and digital technologies for social and cultural theory more consistent with the technical understanding of those most directly working with it — perhaps a more moderate proposition than the doomsday positions taken by some theorists.

What follows moves our attention from a fixation on the 'packaging' surrounding the code, onto the code itself. There is some tendency for researchers to treat technological hardware such as screens, speakers, and other parts of the physical computer apparatus or interface as the primary medium. Studies on the effects of the production and delivery mechanisms of digital code are obviously important, but do not necessarily help us understand the digital text itself. Just as a myriad of physical, mental and emotional attributes come together to form a human being, so too is there a range of physical and metaphysical attributes that contribute to the computers that mediate our binary texts.

The dualist physical versus metaphysical schism that is often used to demarcate and privilege one type of knowledge over another had to be solved theoretically in terms of mathematical logic to make the computer a useful, functioning machine. At the root of this mathematical logic is binary code, which is treated in this work as the digital language (or text). Through binary code, the practical mechanical operations of the machine and the conceptual data it processes are considered not just equal, but actually the same thing in terms of the information they convey. As such, binary code and the algebraic logic by which digital code functions are the focus of this investigation. This thesis argues that there is much more to discover about digital code in terms of the cultural values reflected in its content than many social researchers have thus far elaborated. In so doing, it demonstrates that the cultural values embedded in the code, and thus the possible outcomes we can expect from our continuing technological development, are a completely human creation, with intentional uses and effects that may be intentionally or accidentally disruptive to some social conventions. The cultural values imbued in the technology are conveyed in the design of the medium, or, stated differently, the medium is designed to reflect the cultural values of its inventors. This agency —or intent— in the production of technology is how cultural values are embedded in our inventions.

Embedded in the zeros and ones of digital code is Leibniz's monist philosophy, known as Monadism. Embedded in the circuitry of the computer the code flows through is the rational logic of George Boole. Every time we turn to our computers to process information, in as much as we accept or don't accept what we see on the screen, we put our faith in their prescriptions of the universe and how we should think about it. This faith is no small matter. Boole and Leibniz both rest the accuracy of their inventions of rational philosophic systems on faith in God and the infinite universe. Theirs is a faith that seeks to understand the universe by learning the language of God, which they considered to be what we now call calculus.

It may seem absurd to think of calculus as the language of God, especially given the way it is used by computers with their linear operations and limited, two-symbol vocabulary. None the less, it is the assumption that is built into the computer technology we use. Though rationalists such as Leibniz and Boole sought to explain the universe in its entirety, a critical analysis of their work and digital text resulting from it, shows us the assumptions and values conveyed by the digital code are fully human in their origin. Rather than the language of God, digital code is more accurately described as the human expression of some of the abstract rational processes we use to think. Far from being 'sentient' thinking machines, this code is used in computers and robots to have them mindlessly mimic already programmed human activities or concepts, towards the fulfillment of human goals.

There is no question that the digital language in which much of the world now stores its knowledge is much different than the literary tradition of Western society. The text itself is fluid and process-oriented, as opposed to conveying fixed information. Like chalk on a chalk-board, it is meant to be a temporary display of information. At present it is prone to contestation in terms of both authority and meaning. This shift in dominating medium, and the resulting social and political skirmishes as we come to terms with digital media, is a source of discomfort for some. Still, the machines we as a society create and use tend to perform the way they are meant to, and to be used for exactly what they are designed to do. Just as social motivations give rise to the invention of technology, related social effects come after the fact of its creation, and as history shows, arising dilemmas will be decided according to society's already existing value system. For example, a hammer may be used to hammer things. The things that are acceptable to hammer are socially determined. This doesn't exclude its potential use as a paperweight or a murder weapon, but what distinguishes a hammer as a useful tool is its intentional design to help us strike things better. Any other use is accidental to the use it was intended for (i.e. to hammer nails), or an incidental challenge to already-existing values that will ultimately be the basis of any new social rules arising from such occasions.

The computer was designed to be a machine that calculates at a speed far beyond human comprehension, then translate the results into a language humans can understand. It accomplishes this by using strings of code, or more accurately, electrical pulses. Its employment as a war machine or bank teller and vault is akin to the use of any other tool in the arsenal of human production. The modernist desire to replace human soldiers and workers with machines has a long historical precedent. Inculcated in this are slavery and the moral justification for enslavement, the hierarchical classification of life. This very ancient human conflict betrays the nature of a conflict that imbues the advent of all technology, but is particularly disturbing for some when the goal is the replacement of the human mind.

Many technocrats portray the root source of discomfort with technology as a psychological and/or real battle between humans and the technologies they create. Pop culture is awash with stories of computers challenging humanity for control of the earth's resources, particularly the generation of electricity. In some such stories, humans are actually enslaved by machines and are forced to exist to serve their purposes. Although sensationally enticing, this type of anthropomorphism is misplaced. The actual conflict is between people, and the way technology is used to influence human patterns of relationships. Technologies and machines are created with the intent of promoting or maintaining cultural values, to embody and thereby make their users conform to a codified set of rules. Our inventions are meant to serve people and make the quality of our lives 'better', or at the very least increase leisure time for some. This is often expressed in the ideal of freeing humans from labour, yet in this very notion is embedded a social conflict.

Being freed from labour has been a problematic effect of technology for many centuries, especially for the laborers thereby deprived of income. The fear that we humans can be replaced by machines that are more punctual, more reliable, more accurate, faster, and ultimately more strictly adhere to cultural codes than we who have created them has led to the mechanization of our own human activities. In the interest of efficiency, scientific capitalism has come to require even the most basic of human functions to be examined and adjusted for efficiency. Where possible, fallible human activity is replaced with robotics, or other machines of industrial production. Where outright replacement of people is not possible, human bodies and activity are remade in the image of machines — people are forced to mimic the repetitive and uncreative, yet infinitely devoted and tireless machines that will one day be built to replace them as workers (Wood, 2002: xviii). Given that the mathematical formulas built into computers were supposed by their inventors to be the essence of human thought, this mechanization of human activity also encompasses the human mind.

The fear of machines and the hyperbole of some theorizing about our digital society can thus be very logically explained. Especially since the industrial revolution, human workers have been in competition with machines for our very sustenance, perhaps the most famous illustration of this being the Luddites. The advantages of machines over human workers make them the obvious choice for mundane tasks that can be easily automated. The computer primarily automates the mundane labour of calculating mathematical equations. As illustrated by the example of the hammer, any other use can be considered benignly accidental or a violation of existing values. Specifically offended is that we value ourselves more than our machines.

The computer may very well be a machine that calculates, but the logical circuitry and the code it employs to accomplish this task were invented with a different intent. As the practical fulfillment of Leibniz's vision, the two symbols of the code —zero and one— are supposed to describe the infinite universe for us mortals in terms we can understand. The electronic logic circuits through which this code travels are meant to reflect the full range of possible human logical processes. Taken together, the resulting digital code is intended to express *ad infinitum* the universe and how we as humans may understand it. It is entirely possible to script these operations by hand, though it is painstaking and tedious work. Early electronic computer designs required a great deal of human intervention to produce their results. Prior to such mechanization, human-computing teams in fact performed the calculations mentally and wrote the results by hand. Just as the automated loom 'freed' weavers from their craft, as did the use of slaves 'free' their masters from mundane work, so too did the electronic computer 'free' human computers from their work. Such may be one result of the machine itself, but has the development of calculus and the binary logic used by the computer to process it freed us from needing to think about the universe and God?

It is obvious that to date, humanity has yet to be freed from the 'burden' of thought, and we have not been emancipated from making even very simple decisions on our own behalf. Humanity continues to fret over many of the very same decisions and philosophical quandaries as in Leibniz's time. If anything, by making the infinite range of conceptual possibility in the universe available to the average user, digital technology has made it even more difficult to have faith in the decisions we make. Instead of relying on the dictums of our familial fore-bearers to guide our actions —a proscriptive approach to living— the triumph of rationalism ensures that we scientifically seek the course of action from a range of possibilities with the best odds in our favour. We put our faith in the calculations we believe most likely to benefit us, reducing all teachings to another option among many in our retinue of explanations. However, in so doing, we also unwittingly attach ourselves to the view of the universe elaborated by the rationalists that invented this method of calculation.

In as much as we rely on it for answers, digital code very strongly tells us two things: first, that everything we think we know, physical or otherwise, is illusive abstraction, and second, that even this fact is an illusion subject to mutation and change. Paradoxically, we cannot know anything, except that there is something. Whatever that thing is, we must have faith that it is somehow the best possible thing that can be. Leibniz himself rather arbitrarily and faithfully justified the universe we have as the best of all possible universes, created by God, as a manifestation of His [sic] divine will. In this view, the details of our lives, good or bad, are simply incidental occurrences in the unfolding of a divine plan. What stands out as significant is simply that we as individuals have a part in it at all.

The most prominent critique of Leibniz's postulation came from Voltaire in the form of *Candide*, in which Voltaire illustrates how Leibniz's statement can be easily applied as a simple-minded excuse for any of life's miseries. While Voltaire's scathing refutation of Leibniz's statement provides grounds for a lively argument, it doesn't change the fact that when all is said and done, it is Leibniz's logic that we put our faith in every time we rely on a computer. Binary digital code reflects the instability of informational details, looking instead to processes for a sense of stability. To use the analogy of travel, we do not trust our maps nor the road, and neither our mode of transportation. Rather, we trust that we move from one place to another. Our transportation technologies are subject to change, but the process of travel remains a constant in human existence. The route may not always be considered the most direct or the fastest, but we do tend to believe we choose the best of all possible routes towards our final destination.

Leibniz's vision of the universe is one in which process takes precedence over information, mutation over permanence, emphasizing individual experience. A practical example, electronic word-processing has displaced the relative permanence of writing in the digital era. As Voltaire was quick to point out, ignoring the details of life can have the effect of trivializing the major events and catastrophes that we often think of as comprising the significance of life itself. This monadism when taken to its logical relativist extreme can be read as solipsism, in which one considers only one's own self as existing and one's own thoughts and activities as important. Since truth is only found in process, the process of being oneself is the only truth we can know, and even this only by the fact of doing rather than knowing. We are thereby only defined as humans by our actions that distinguish us from infinite other possible definitions, just as the computer is defined by its ability to process binary code and compute. The results of computation and the code itself are conflated into making up the whole of the machine — neither they nor the machine exist independent of one another. Interpreted through Leibniz, replacing human activity with machines challenges our most fundamental but erroneous way of knowing ourselves (as tangible entities), and also threatens to reveal our most fundamental sense of being (as ceaselessly changing). This is the case for Leibniz because we cannot exist independent of the things we think and do and experience — we cannot simply rip the mind from the body, nor the body from the mind. However, in response to the replacement of human thought by machine, wisdom is more than just calculation, and being human involves more activity than just thinking.

As already affirmed, since we humans are the authentic 'thing' upon which machine designs are based, regardless of their sophistication, machines are only imitations of what we have already determined possible and/or desirable. As intended, binary digital code only helps describe us and the universe to ourselves, in a way we can already understand. To attribute any more is as baseless as attributing a carpenter's misplaced blow to their hammer. Machines are not motivated. Humans are clearly the motivation for our machine's existence and activities and the power behind them.

To be fair, misunderstanding digital technology is easy. Though it represents a logic most humans are thought to possess, it is presented to us in such a way as to mystify its underlying characteristics. What follows illustrates some of the fundamental features of digital technology: how it was built, how it functions, and what meaning binary code represents in terms of both denotation and connotation. The focus is centered on the aspects productive of the code, describing its invention and the ideas assumed in its rhetoric. I wish to affirm from the outset that binary code as we use it in 'digital' society is firmly rooted in the computer. Though they are not entirely the same, either one is useless without the other. Like our human mind is embodied in the brain, binary code is embodied in the computer, so that it is necessary to understand both in order to understand either on its own. Beginning in the next section with a more complete description of how cultural values are understood in relation to our inventions, the characteristics of binary code as we now know and experience it are then laid out. The sections following that describe two general areas productive of the text that can be described first as the material/historical aspects that produced the machine, followed by the logical/philosophical arguments that make the digital text meaningful beyond a purely technical explanation.

00001 About Cultural Values

The emergence of our 'digital' civilization (the electronic stock market with its digital currency, internet, cellular telecommunications, desktop digital imaging etc.) is happening at a time of other social upheavals, such as Globalization and the dominance of neoliberal economics, the emergence of 'globalized' (or at least 'internationalized') resistance movements such as anti-globalization, environmentalism, the extremism of international terror, and the more mundane but no less radical call for an international digital clock. With reference to the work of Harold Innis, we can assume that our society is adjusting to accommodate the proliferation and preservation of its chosen dominant medium of communication. This raises some poignant questions as regards the 'real' influence of digital media in changing relations of power and the way we generally think. One might suggest it is not always so simple as just a cause and effect relationship, but it can also be contended that digital media is sure to produce *some* directly attributable effects, which are, after all, the reason technologies are invented in the first place. This being the case, a good understanding of the epistemic assumptions —the cultural values guiding thought— built into the primary medium of the digital computer code is required if we are to formulate a sensible understanding of the technologies built upon it:

> once a technology is admitted, it plays out its hand; it does what it is designed to do. Our task is to understand what that design is — that is to say, when we admit a new technology to the culture, we must do so with our eyes wide open. (Postman, 1992: 7)

The present changes in our civilization connected with the advent of digital information are consistent with the pattern of technologically inspired upheavals in the past (as elaborated by Innis, 1986). It should not come as much of a surprise that we are going through social changes —in particular, arguments about authenticity, property and authority— at this time when our dominant mode of information storage is changing. This shift is probably most public in court battles over property rights associated with the code. For example, the famous case of the recording industry against Napster file-sharing software can be understood on its most basic level as being about control over duplication and movement of binary code. In a converse case, Microsoft has been shown to have limited the types of software that would function with their operating system, granting themselves a monopoly over most of the world's personal computers. Again, this is an issue primarily over control of the binary code that is the life-blood of computer technology and the computer software industry, and decisions in this regard are being sorted out according to our existing cultural values.

Innis describes how modes of communication influence entire civilizations by affecting their structures of power relations, which are rooted in their knowledge base (1991: 3). Seeming to pick up on Francis Bacon's sentiment, "For knowledge... is itself power," Innis helps us understand shifts of power to be rather

14

complexly interconnected communications phenomena. Those who possess the dominant mode (or medium) of communication control society. Possession in this sense means the control of all things concerned with manufacturing and defining what is considered "knowledge." This product of communication becomes the possession of those who control its (re)production, who use it as a tool to exert power and control over populations.

From Innis' point of view, a useful dualist model of communication systems puts oral tradition on one side, against "literate" tradition on the other. These two modes of communication could then be associated to further binary differences, such as class differentials, time/space concerns, etc. with one side clearly belonging to a privileged group with the capacity to exert control over the other as described above. The dominant form of communication will always have a bias that can be understood to concern itself with either obliterating distance by emphasizing time sensitivity, and thus binding society across space, or conversely, unifying society through time by emphasizing spatial sensitivity. He posits that the prolonged dominance of either type of given medium affects knowledge to the point of creating a new civilization, in that the term "knowledge" comes to be defined by a worldview which is ultimately shaped by the medium itself. To ensure their survival, groups marginalized by whichever mode of communication dominates form an opposition to that dominating medium and thereby oppose the dominating power structure. They do this by cultivating an oppositionally biased medium (entailing a different use of language or different language altogether) that eventually grows to displace that and those formerly in control.

In spite of its attraction, it is erroneous to think of binary code as simply a reflection of the popular conception of binary opposites, like the above Innisian perspective. Binary code uses zero and one as the symbols of its entire number system, and these symbols stand no more in opposition to each other that any two letters of the English alphabet. One may be habitually inclined to think of one and zero in the context of a sports score, entailing a winner and a loser in opposition with each other. This literal reading of binary code emphasizes a Cartesian dualist philosophical perspective in which '0' signifies nothing and '1' signifies something specific, as the machine interprets it. However, behind the literal reading is connoted a Leibnitizian monist perspective in which the entire universe of infinite possibility exists, and '1' signifies the existence and arbitrary recognition of a specific category of things from that limitless pool of possibility. Rather than signifying one choice versus no choice, the term 'binary' as it is used in computer technology signifies a vast pool of things, from which one type of thing is selected. Thus, in terms of politics, a more accurate analysis of digital code accounts for the maintenance and/or displacement of power positions vis-a-vis one another, not as the simple dominance of one individual or group over another.

With this understanding, the worldview promoted by digital code does appear to contest popular Western notions of how power and authority should and do manifest. In the case of power disruptions attributable to digital code, though its birth came about as a military project, countless actors in our contemporary civilization are assuring its position as our information storage medium of choice. Corporate interests have displaced the military as the main developer of digital hardware, but at the same time, public citizens develop some of the most ingenious software as 'open source' code. It is thus difficult to discern a clear opposition between two conflicting parties the way Innis' work suggests we should be able to, even though the dominating power structure is under pressure at least in part inspired by our shift to digital technology.

This provides rich grounds for speculation regarding inter-cultural communication, but the focus of this thesis is investigating the digital code that is now used to store our knowledge in contemporary western civilization, be it highly controlled corporate or military information, or public open-source material. The central point here is investigating what digital code reveals about itself as an information storage medium, not comparing and contrasting various modes of communication thought to be in competition with each other. Even so, it is important that we begin with notions of power and knowledge foremost in our minds, lest we forget the lived experiences that are the everyday concerns of humanity. The strongest point we can pick up from Innis is his underlying affirmation of intent regarding communication technology. Every invention has its intended uses and effects built into it. Digital code and the mathematical processes that make it meaningful are no less so.

For Innis knowledge is a product of social interaction, more succinctly described as communication. Similarly, post-modernist Jean-Francois Lyotard describes knowledge as a game played out in language guided by and legitimating the dominating rules of logic (1996: 435). Knowledge is the possession of those who control its (re)production (or 'discourse' in postmodernist terminology), and it is used by them as a means of asserting power and control. Knowledge is most simply a 'language game' that is guided by a particular type of logic. Resistance to the dominating class in this context comes from destabilizing the rules (or logic) that control the discourse. In Lyotard's opinion, the "computerization" (conversion of our knowledge base into digital code) of the West affects knowledge in our civilization to the point of creating social upheaval. Redefinition of the rules of discourse is a moment of terror for the Western world. In this view, power struggles over former definitions of social codes, such as property and ownership, are ultimately over the power to enclose the digital code as another private domain, and thereby try to force it to fit already existing definitions of property.

The findings of this thesis show that the code in our computers resists traditional notions of enclosure in at least two ways. On a literal level, the mechanical apparatus necessary to mediate the code requires a very high level of redundancy, meaning that virtually any binary code string should be crackable. On a more philosophical level, binary code highlights the arbitrary nature of all definition, indicating a clear target for those inclined to challenge notions of authority. These observations impel a better description of the relationship between the machinery and the code.

As mentioned above, it seems that much social theorizing about digital technology has tended towards a fixation on the tools of encoding and interpretation themselves, and the social acts of mass or interpersonally mediated communication. Such work often describes the mechanical appendages of the code as tools extending human capacities (as described in Marshal McLuhan's work, 1964: 23-24), but ignores the implications of how the code itself may give shape to possible lived or imagined experiences and thus shape our ways of knowing the world. McLuhan furthered Innis's idea that the dominant form of communication reveals the defining features of society by examining the implications of technology on a macro-social level. McLuhan was interested in the way that media structure human experiences and processes from a more subjective stance. Operating with a definition of "media" which can be summed up as 'conveyers of meaning' (conveyers of other media), and from the premise that media basically function to "amplify" or "extend" human capacities, he states his task to be investigating media's social effects. The key here is that the "content" of the media is not the message for McLuhan, but rather the message is "the change of scale or pace or pattern that it introduces into human affairs" (McLuhan, 1964: 24). Content

18

can be thought of as the literal reading of the message being mediated, while the broader social implications are a result of the practices of using the medium. In the case of digital media, it is most often the interpretive devices under investigation, not the code which they mediate, which is often arbitrarily disregarded as the insignificant 'content' in McLuhan's terminology.

Since it is through media that people extend themselves through time and space, a given medium itself structures the very way people think of extending in time and space. McLuhan thus states that "the medium is the message" because it is the way that media structure experience (or thought, as the case may be) that is the important part of any medium, which may be very different from the "content" the medium is conveying. He gives us the example of electric light, which is usually perceived as having no message because by itself, a single light bulb has no content. However, in spite of its lack of content, the light bulb does produce a change in the structure of human activity by making space conquerable through the obliteration of the night/day cycle.

In keeping with McLuhan's theorizing, contemporary digital media produce a change in how even those without direct access to the technology think of the world. For example, I have noticed a popular notion among my novice students of computer literacy that computers themselves are smart, and people are not — it is also assumed that people make mistakes, and computers don't. Thus, information coming from a computer is perceived as more credible than that from a human source, and humans are perceived as needing computers to exist in the contemporary world. Many computer illiterate people seem to consider their own discomfort with computer technology a justification for notions of their own diminished importance in the present labour economy.

Changes in the way seasoned users think of the world also result from digital technology. For example, a document such as this thesis may be constructed through numerous 'cut and paste' edits until its flow agrees with the author's aesthetic sensibility. The result of this possibility is that the writing process is no longer simply a continuous narrative process, as it might once have been when editing was more labour intensive. Outlining and various other preparatory work that is very important when one is writing by hand or typewriter may have less emphasis when working with digital text, and corrections and the editorial process itself become mainly the work of the author.

McLuhan's analysis of technology as the extension of human capacity is the perspective adopted by the creators of the electronic computer, much as the logical models behind the circuitry were intended by their authors to describe and improve our rational methods. However, there is a danger in adopting only this limited perspective that may lead to technological determinist hyperbole. For example, consider the following:

> uncontrolled growth of technology destroys the vital sources of our humanity. It creates a culture without a moral foundation. It undermines certain mental processes and social relations that make human life worth living (Postman, 1992: xii).

It would seem we are in a rather hopeless position indeed if human life is no longer even worth living as the result of technological change, since all indications are that technological development is continuing to proliferate at an astounding rate. Further, one might well ask whether it is possible for a culture to exist without a moral code. Rather than succumb to such hysteria, we must acknowledge that technology does inspire some change in cultural values, but with the understanding that the values spread through technology are no less a human creation than those displaced. It cannot be emphasized enough that, for example, the obliteration of the night/day cycle with electric light is precisely the intended result, not an accident. Likewise, many of the disruptions accompanying digital technology —such as the displacement of people from their labours— are intentional.

Cultural Values and Machines

Cultural values are generally assumed to signify the social code of right and wrong conduct, and this is the way it is to be understood here. In addition to physical conduct, cultural values also refer to the way we think. In more theological terminology, it can be discussed as both orthodoxy and orthopraxy — the correct way to think and the right way to do things. Cultural values are, of course, humanly constructed, and enter into everything we think and do, when both alone and in groups. They demarcate both what is acceptable and what is not. Our values are a part of our everyday conduct such that we may not often think of them as anything other than normal, self-obviating ways of doing things. A value system is thus a ubiquitous source of authority in any society, and those who are privileged as the definers and interpreters of values have a position of great advantage over others in terms of power; that is, the ability to have their way even when others are opposed. The most obvious historical example of such an authority in Western society is the Christian church, though as a contemporary institution the state justice system presents a serious challenge to church authority, in that the state alone possesses the ultimate power of enforcement. Values can thus be understood as constantly monitored and enforced, even if they are subject to negotiation and change from time to time.

Bruno Latour (1992) encourages us to ask what values we build into (or embed in) the machines that we create to serve us. Even something so mundane as the invention of the eraser on the end of a pencil reveals that in authorship we expect mistakes, but that even when erased, a trace of one's fallibility remains behind.

21

Equally so, a wheelchair access ramp may be read as an expression of the ideal of equality, or the absence of such a ramp, erasure of a lived experience. Along these lines, Andrew Feenberg writes, "Machines are comparable to texts because they too inscribe a story, i.e. a prescribed sequence of events which the user initiates and undergoes" (Feenberg, 1998). Through its circuitry, computers inscribe the stories and ideas of numerous logicians from the past several centuries (Davis, 2000: xii). Binary code is the expression of that collection of logic. In addition to functionalist extensions of human capacities, digital technology also expresses human logic rooted in the cultural values of the machines' operations. In the case of binary code, this root can be traced back to the logic and values of Leibniz's vision and his justification of it, monadism.

The body of this thesis shows in greater detail how the philosophy of Leibniz is built into the electronic computer. Here, I will simply affirm that this entails for us in the contemporary world the privileging of algebra and mathematics as the highest expression of human thought. Not only this, but that rational human thought is considered always a linear procedure, which in turn enables machines to process complex information —that is, to rationalize— much faster than humans. Speed is privileged over patience, and understanding gives way to blind faith in the machine's calculations.

The theories informing technological innovations influence the way we think of the human mind (Manovich, 1995: 5), and the machines incorporating those theories are taken as evidence of theoretical validity. Analysis of digital code reveals that the emergence of our 'digital' civilization is not the limitless expanse of possibility it is popularly labeled, but rather a different set of limits on our ways of knowing the world. In terms of values, it is a re-demarcation of the right way for humans to think and act. The philosophical works on logic by Leibniz and Boole that are the basis of computer engineering are exactly the theoretical paradigms referred to here. Both logicians were concerned with creating theoretical models of the workings of the human mind, and this mind metaphor found its expression in the physical layout and wiring of the computer's various components, which was designed with the human brain as its blueprint. To be blunt, altogether, the logicians and the engineers that contributed to the creation of the electronic computer across the ages thought they were in some way making a human mind. For many, the computer itself may be considered proof of the triumph of mind over matter, or science over nature, but perhaps irrationalists will have this final say.

The dualism represented by the 'science vs. nature' schism got the computer built but, ironically, embedding in it a logic that Horkheimer and Adorno characterize as "irrationalism" made it possible for it to exist in its present form (1995: 91). As they point out, while fully utilizing rationalist methods, Leibniz's philosophical work ultimately rests on a foundation of 'Truth' found in the irrationality of emotions, not in the rational logic of his own philosophy. In a similar twist, Boole appeals to monotheistic faith to provide the final justification for his work, not the test of his own logic against itself. The man who demonstrated the way to work Boole's logic into electronic circuitry, Claude Shannon, also makes an irrational appeal —this time to intuition— to support his assumptions. According to the methods elaborated by both Leibniz and Boole, any conclusion not arrived at through reason is not rational. So within the electronic computer itself there is this contradiction: the outward appearance of the hardware (machinery) representing a triumph of Cartesian dualism, while the software (code) without which the machinery is useless represents an assertion of monadism, in which faith in the infinite determines all 'things' are essentially equal. One might wittingly remark, "It thinks, therefore it is, but what strange thoughts it has—it doesn't seem to care at all what it says!" In the end, the two components can only be theoretically separated from each other, since either component is useless without the other.

Here I suggest that much of the present social phenomena attributable to digital media can be considered a reflection of the contradiction that the machine presents to us as users. As intended, the cosmology of monism contests popular notions rooted in dualism such as 'good vs. evil' are being upset by the 'all things are equal' value inscribed in the code of the technology we use. As a practical example, moral restrictions on sexuality based on age are under strain in the context of internet technology, where free pornographic code is easily accessible to any user. Even the popular understanding of the numbers '0' and '1' are upset by the fact of how the code works. In Boolean database searches, entering '0' instructs the machine to report everything in a category, while '1' makes it report a specific thing. I propose that what lays behind the presently emerging situation are a different set of rationalist principles, rules and concepts that displace those which we popularly know. This may feel unstable and threatening to some, but in response to such hyperbole as the example above, one can hardly consider it the end of "human life worth living."

Does the computer really represent the human mind and how we think? The answer for this thesis is a compromise: only to the extent that we rely on computers to 'think' for us, it is safe to say yes, this is how we think. That extent may be quantified to varying degrees in different circumstances and settings. Here it is enough to recognize that machines do play an intentional role (to whatever degree of success) in how we think of ourselves and our world and universe. The computer is *meant* to influence our way of knowing, and binary code is *meant* to communicate monist rationalism. It should be no surprise to us that they do exactly what their inventors intended.

00010 Description of Binary Text

In 1938 Claude Shannon[1] wrote what Herman Goldstine[2] is widely quoted as judging "one of the most important master's theses ever written" (Goldstine, 1993: 119-120). Indeed, it was a decisive moment in the seeming triumph of rationalism over the 'natural' world. Shannon's paper demonstrated how George Boole's (1864) algebraic expression of what he considered the complete logical workings of the human mind could be applied to electronic circuitry, through the use of different types of electrical switches. It had been two centuries since Leibniz proposed his idea that calculus could describe the universe — the operations later elaborated by Boole — and his belief that a 'thinking machine' could be built that could automatically perform the calculations.[3] While it is questionable whether a machine that fully thinks is in

---

[1] Considered the founder of 'Information Theory', inventor of the word 'bit' (binary digit) and, with Warren Weaver, originator of the 'transmission' model of communications.

[2] Co-inventor and project coordinator of the world's first full-scale electronic digital computer, the ENIAC, and its successor, the EDVAC. Also, President Emeritus of the American Philosophical Society.

[3] Leibniz himself succeeded in building a small calculating machine, though its function was not fully automated.

fact possible,[4] Shannon's engineering know-how combined with Boole's propositions regarding the workings of the human mind has a continuing revolutionary effect on human communication, perception and knowledge. Regarding his incredible accomplishment, Shannon is quoted as attributing it to an accident of history: "It just happened that no one else was familiar with both fields at the same time" (Redshaw, 2001).

Shannon's modesty aside, there is no doubt about the historical impact his engineering breakthrough has had on the direction of technological evolution since. The fruition of Shannon's thesis, the EDVAC (Electronic Discrete Variable Calculator) came into existence in 1950 as the result of a massive engineering and financial effort. Every computer built since the EDVAC has been based on its design, referred to as "von Neumann architecture," after the famous mathematician John von Neumann[5] who collaborated with Goldstine and numerous others who designed and created the first two full-scale electronic programmable computers. Of course, embedded into the von Neumann design is the use of Boolean logic expressed as binary code. This is physically realized through the so-called 'hard-wiring' of the code into the computer circuitry. I will here describe how these innovations combine in the computer to form a text written in binary code.

As many are aware, the zeros and ones of binary code are the most fundamental aspect of computers. Strings of code made entirely of zeros and ones — based on a technique of code writing invented by logician Alan Turing[6] — are the logical algebraic

---

[4] Whether such a machine is desirable is almost irrelevant at this historical moment, since countless corporations and inventors have made it their purpose to turn such a vision into reality.

[5] More infamously known as one of the key figures in the invention of the atomic bomb.

[6] In mathematics and logic, famous as the inventor of the 'Turing Machine' among other spectacular achievements; perhaps most

expression of all things entered, stored, and generated by computers. Zeros and ones represent the primary text of all modern computers, and as such, form the primary text of all things that employ computer circuitry, from coffee makers to satellites.

What is a 'Binary' text?

In purely technical terms, a binary computer text can be described as a 'discrete' series of binary digits (named 'bits' by Shannon) used to form 'words' (aka bytes) which describe the location of the information for storage and retrieval within the computer system, instructions telling the computer processor what to do with the information, and the information itself. In more colloquial terms, a label that contains its intended address and instructions for handling accompanies each bit of information.

The term 'discrete' in this explanation means that the stream of code expresses only one full digit of value at a time (also referred to as discontinuous values), and thus, in the case of binary code, nothing more or less than the full interval values of either '0' or '1'. This can be contrasted with the analog equivalent, which is called a 'continuous' signal because it may display all information between any arbitrary intervals. For example, there are values between zero and one such as '0.333...' that can be expressed continuously, but not discretely (thus necessitating the '...' sign to tell us that the number is arbitrarily halted at that cutoff point).

Another example of this is the analog wristwatch, whose hands may point not only at the numbers on the face but also the spaces in between. This can be contrasted with a digital watch,

---

popularly famous now as a master code-breaker for the British during WWII, which was previously not widely known due to the 'top secret' nature of his work at that time.

which only displays one full minute value at a time, displaying no intervals in between.

Human sense perception is analog in nature, but by flooding our senses with enough discreet digits, we can be said to experience a simulation of an analog experience. For example, assuming this page you are reading is printed on a digital printer, the letters are made of numerous small ink dots that appear solid to the human eye. Anna Munster terms this an "approximate aesthetic" experience, where 'aesthetic' is understood to mean human sensation (Munster, 2001). Human interpretation is thus shown to be analog, and, in linguistic terms, every digital signifier connotes meaning analogically:

> One of the most notable digital codes is writing. Writing is predominantly digital because each character is discrete. As Derrida likes to point out, the letter 'e' is either the letter 'e' or it isn't. However, in spite of this apparent precision at the level of the character, how writing creates meaning is not so simple. ...there is always an analogue level to digital expression. (Chesher, 2002)

Chesher explains that the term 'digital' has become fetishized in the contemporary context to signify anything related to computer technology, which is actually misleading. The von Neumann design 'digital' computer in fact uses only two discrete digits in its circuitry and logical operations, '0' or '1', implying the term 'binary' should be included in every reference to this type of digital text. Unless otherwise stated in this thesis, the terms 'binary' or 'digital' will be used interchangeably to refer to binary digital computer code. This leads to the issue of where this code can be found.

Human sensory and sense-making experiences happen analogically — whether we intend to or not, we believe in the solidity of what we see and experience. Although early programs were written in binary code form, for many decades now strings of binary code are seldom if ever seen by human computer users, be they normal users or even specialists. If binary code is actually handled by humans — perhaps for educational purposes — it is still abstracted to the textual representation of zeros and ones so humans can understand it. Text is actually used in computers as a "metalanguage" (Manovich, 2002: 74). The binary code itself exists on a sub-atomic scale, in the form of charged electrons: "The bulk of written texts ... do not exist anymore in perceivable time and space but in a computer memory's transistor cells" (Kittler, 1995). The physical manifestation of digital code is on a scale far too small for humans to usefully access without sophisticated interfacing devices, including hardware such as keyboards and screens, and software such as programming language translators. The interfacing and translating devices change the rapidly pulsating code into an approximate aesthetic that humans can understand, such as the zeros and ones of binary code. Where 'zero' and 'one' philosophically represent complex logical arguments, binary digits in literal technological language represent simply a flow of electrical charges. 'One' means there is a pulse of electricity, and 'zero' signifies that there is a pause between pulses. Various combinations of these two symbols in binary code correspond with closed (on) or open (off) switches in the logical circuit arrays (Selvia, 1995). This physical function refutes the popular notion of binary as signifying two opposites, because in physical space the phenomenon is actually about movement on a subatomic scale. The direction of the flow of electricity is the issue; the human concept of competition has no part in such a phenomenon.

Understood as the movement of electrons, digital text is thus process oriented, not a fixed or static entity (Godfrey in Innis, 1986: 173). Like any living language, digital code is dynamic, not static. Sound works heard in live performance serve as a clear analogy to the dynamic processes of digital text. However, the dynamic nature of live music is such that no two performances will be exactly the same; each performance is uniquely different from other performances of the very same piece. This is not the case in the digital realm, where a dynamic process can theoretically be re-performed as an original performance, though it might be quantitatively identical to infinite others. The contradiction of a re-performance being at the same time original indicates a challenge to the rules of authenticity and originality. At the very least, understanding the digital 'narrative' process requires understanding its dynamism to include the processing of theoretically perfect reproductions of works.

The concept of scale modeling is a convenient metaphor for understanding the way binary code operates in its raw electrical form. The idea of representation through miniaturization is historically common. In 1945 Vannever Bush hypothesized a system of knowledge storage that would be based on miniaturized film (comparable to micro-fiche), predicting with remarkable accuracy concepts such as hyper-linking now used in web page designs, and the freedom of movement now enjoyed by the use of ever smaller technologies that improve on portability. Though his favored storage medium was incorrect, his description of miniaturizing texts to the point that they would be useless without ultra-mediation was completely in keeping with the reduction of information to binary digital storage, and its (re)magnification to a scale useable by humans. The resulting digital text is a "discrete and synthetic microworld image of the original problem" (Hasslacher in Kittler, 1995).

Aside from its scale, another unique feature of this text is its basis in motion. Even though the computer circuitry through which it flows is not changeable, the code pulsing through the hardwiring is. A reasonable analogy to this can again be found in music (referring to the physical domain of sound, which itself is the movement of particles in air), where there may perhaps be only one instrument playing one tone, but with limitless rhythmic possibilities. In the hands of a skilled performer, such a composition can still easily convey emotion. However, this analogy fails once again when it comes to the issue of speed, because the computer performs at a rate that is beyond human conceptual imagination.

The ultra-mediated inscription of binary code requires an inputting device to control the mechanical parts of the process. This gives rise to two distinct phenomenological origins of digital text. The first type of text can be thought of as originating inside the circuitry of the machine. This type of text is constructed entirely from the workings of the machine and its software, meaning the electrons that are arranged on the storage drive are the first representation of the text constructed. An electronic music composition with all its waveforms created on the machine is such a text.

The second type of digital text originates outside the machine, and requires a device to 'digitize' the analog information. A photograph —digital, or otherwise a scanned print photo— is an example of this type of text, where there is a distinct origin outside the computer. It is not possible in this case to discuss the binary scale-model as the original thing. Nonetheless, once the data is scanned and input, the information may be worked upon to the point that the 'original' thing is no longer recognizable.

In either of these two possible origins, the distinction is for the most part only theoretical. Generally speaking, neither the resulting digital code nor the (re)enlargement of it contains any humanly discernable aesthetic evidence that tells what gave rise to that particular pattern of electrons. This is one of three types of disruptions to popular notions of authenticity

The second disruption to textual authenticity is the exact duplication 'copy and paste' technique of composition that code easily facilitates, and usually incorporates in the creation of programs. With copy and paste being a normal part of digital composition (especially in programming), binary code is an open text that is always undergoing the process of (re)construction. The exact same code strings are duplicated, modified, and/or moved from one location to another without degeneration, and without limit. Such a text is never complete: "[there is] no act of closure for a data file" (Rodowick, 2001: 212). The way we work with binary code does not allow for closure the way the conclusiveness of print does. This process defies naming an individual author, and neither is it stable in terms of completion. Once it exists, not only is it impossible to discern with confidence where the code came from, it is also impossible to say with confidence when and by whom it was first produced.[7]

Benjamin discusses the notion of authenticity as dependent on the origin of a piece of work from a unique time and place:

> The authenticity of a thing is the essence of all that is transmissible from its beginning, ranging from its substantive duration to its testimony to the history which it has experienced. Since the historical testimony rests on

---

[7] Techniques for registering such features are now being developed as the result of rampant pirating of digital information, most notoriously the case of Napster file sharing. Even so, the battle to claim authenticity is far from over, as file-sharing software continues to evolve and evade both detection and regulation. Complicating our understanding of the issue, there has in fact been legal approval of a copyright claim for specific algorithms in the United States (Kittler 1995). Technically, it can be said that the intensity of these legal battles is such because the nature of binary code itself makes it easy to copy perfectly and without limit, and that it will ultimately be very difficult if not impossible to put a halt to file sharing.

the authenticity, the former, too, is jeopardized by reproduction when substantive duration ceases to matter. (Benjamin, 1969: 221)

The digital text defies popular notions of both time and space, and thus defies traditional notions of authenticity. Not only is its origin unknowable, digital text does not degenerate like other artifacts, implying a further reconceptualization of time-scale, and presenting us with the third disruption of traditional authenticity. If there is no degeneration, its moment of genesis is neither discernable nor historically important to the text in and of itself.

The implications of this in terms of property and ownership are a strong concern that has inspired much controversy and investigation. Binary code is theoretically a free-floating system of representation, like Baudrillard's notion of simulacra. If the sub-atomic scale-models made of electrons are purely representative, their human-scale projections are theoretically even more so. Rather than get caught in Baudrillard's endless chain of false representation, there is a convenient way to arbitrarily assert the existence of this text which we will never actually see: by treating the representation as real in and of itself (Massumi, 1987). This may be read as an arbitrary, technocratic solution, and not without its problems, but it is a convenient one for this thesis in that it allows the code to be treated as something tangible. If originality cannot be discerned based on a prior location in time and space, then we must take the thing as it is as something no less real than the electrons of which it is comprised. If based on our faith in science we accept that electrons are real even though we cannot see them, then we must accept that the code as it has been described thus far exists. Accepting this is made easier by the fact of the architecture of the computer circuitry, which we can to some extent analogically see and touch in the form of computer chips.

The series of switches and circuits that make up the hard wiring of the computer have evolved incredibly since the use of vacuum tubes in the first electronic computer. Like sub-atomic canals, the microscopic wiring of contemporary computer chips provides the infrastructure for the movement of information. In this complex and unimaginably fast moving maze, there is neither room for confusion nor error. At the level of the text itself, the coding must be clear and unambiguous. This mathematical language within the machine is "non-rhetorical," since it is a text that cannot be argued with (Manovich, 2002: 77). The rhetoric of this type of text began and ended centuries ago with the writing of Leibniz's philosophy. There is no place for conceptual debates or ambiguity in the literal digital text, as confusion only leads to immediate and devastating breakdowns in the flow of information, also known as crashes. On the linguistic level, the writing of binary code is purely indexical, where the sign is understood to signify something else, although the index is severely limited. The indexical interpretation of zero and one in the digital context might very well read "this way" and "that way." Marshall McLuhan can help us understand this type of medium.

McLuhan explains media as belonging either to a "hot" or "cold" category, depending on what he perceived to be their required "involvement" from the audience of a given medium (McLuhan, 1964: 36). Hot media, such as literature, require less participation from the audience than cold media does, because hot media have "high definition," meaning that they convey a lot of information. In contrast, the "low definition" cold media, such as television, require the audience to actively complete the messages being inferred. According to McLuhan's schematic, digital technology is a "hot" medium, transporting more information to and from individuals at a faster rate than ever before. As I have described it, digital code is completely unintelligible without another technology with which to encode or decode the content, which are themselves the means of interface for individual users. The code and the machine are in this regard physically inseparable from one another. As research and development produce ever-faster techniques of processing digital code, the experience of using the technology requires less and less participation from the user— the machinery does the hard work for us. As anyone who works with computers can attest (particularly working with large database programs), it seems that more time can be spent typing simple commands and waiting for the machines to work than in actually engaging with the information.

Moving outside the closed context of the machine, I do take issue with the concept that binary code is completely 'non-rhetorical'. It may be true that the code severely limits the interpretive possibilities for the machine's various devices, but this is just its literal reading. Barthes writes, "a system which takes over the signs of another system in order to make them its signifiers is a system of connotation ... the literal image is *denoted* and the symbolic image is *connoted*" (Barthes, 1988: 37). As we've seen, the only possible literal reading of binary code is by machines. On the human scale, the meaning is connoted through various "approximate aesthetics." The connotative aspect of the text forms a rhetoric that affirms an ideology. Because of this, one can analyze this text for meaning beyond its functional aspects, and distinguish connoted social values.

In contrast with literal meaning, connotative meaning is a product of inference in the processes of both production and reception (Barthes: 19). Connoted meaning may not be immediately recognized like literal meaning is. Exposing connoted meaning requires a detailed investigation of the cultural knowledge at work in the various constituents of the message. The materiality and the theoretical aspects of digital code point to a number of issues that need clarification in this regard.

00011 The Interface: The languages of software

Ironically, achieving the mechanical goal of "speeding up human processes" (Goldstine, 1993: 47) requires tremendous abstraction from the actual human processes themselves. When the average user looks at an average computer terminal, the last things one is apt to think of are the actual processes that are happening in the circuitry. This is no accident. Rather than deal with the machine on its own technical terms, users 'interface' with the technology through a much more familiar and easier to use set of protocols: "on an intentionally superficial level, perfect graphic user interfaces, since they dispense with writing itself, hide a whole machine from its users" (Kittler, 1995). The machine being hidden is very simply describable as a machine that produces mathematical algorithms, which are then interpreted for human use. Various levels of languages between the algorithmic text and the user level of interaction, such as word-processing, obscure the fact that what is abstractly represented are mathematical processes, not static text (Godfrey in Innis, 1986: 173). Not only do computer users not see or understand the processes of the code that they work through the interface, but the speed at which it operates it is completely unintelligible on a real (human) time scale anyway.

Extension of the human capacity for thought is equal to (or limited by) the ability of humans to interface usefully with the machine (Rokeby, 1995: 149). Since the machine actually performs millions of calculations per second, the interface is a means of making it seem like the machine has slowed down enough for humans to actually use it. It wasn't always this way. The first electronic computer actually required a human programmer to manually set the switches to direct the information flows correctly. However, even by the invention of the second electronic computer it was realized that the machine itself could set its own program switches much faster and more accurately than a human could. It is now impossible to conceive of a computer without this 'stored program' system, referring to the sets of coded instructions stored in the computer's memory (more widely known as software). The process is so evolved at this point that, as any user knows, clicking a pictorial icon has replaced typed commands. While this innovation allows almost everyone to use a computer in one way or another, it should also be remembered that there are numerous other seemingly banal applications of computer technology that provide even less opportunity for users to interact with the code.

How does one interface with the computer in their coffee-maker? Or in one's vacuum cleaner? Or even in their automobile engine? The answers are, of course, by making coffee, by vacuuming dirt, and by driving — by doing what we normally do, only with some computationally enhanced result. This simplicity serves to remind that the performance of the intended act is the limit built into computer technology, and no further coding is desirable in many cases. Nevertheless, even the most basic computer chips need to be reset from time to time, and it is in those moments that we come to realize that the act of switching on the appliance is first and foremost a moment of initiating a computer program.

The difference between what I will call these 'passive' programs and the interactive ones such as the word processor being used to type this thesis, is the ability to manipulate the code being produced. The word manipulate is important here, as it may be taken to suggest *man*agement of the data, or *man*ually working the code to some degree. Where a coffee-maker computer may simply monitor the temperature fluctuations of the hotplate through built-in sensors, the human interface computer is meant to present intelligibly at least some of the internal possibilities of the machine to the user. Access to the code is a limit on the type of experience users may have (Rokeby, 1995: 145).

Just as any mathematical problem requires the use of pen and paper to calculate manually the result, binary operations now entail the modern computer interface. This can be distinguished as the "cultural interface," wherein the terminology reflects the way human-computer interfaces are based on cultural forms we already understand (Manovich, 2002: 70-71). This can be contrasted with a machine interface, which is a purely technical issue and doesn't require a human/cultural interpretive process beyond writing the initial program (Manovich: 93). It may be tempting to consider the interface the "real medium of a computer" as Manovich does, because it is at that level that human meaning is read. While this is certainly a valid rationale, it doesn't recognize that human meaning can also be read at a much more base level — the level at which it is encoded. His is as arbitrary a determination as this present investigation treating binary code as the primary text, with particular cultural values embedded in it. Even so, from Manovich can be taken his assertion that the cultural interface must come in a format familiar enough to users for them to usefully access, through various program languages, the circuitry inside the box. The most common manifestation of this type of interface is called the GUI (graphical user interface).

First appearing in Macintosh computers in 1984, the GUI changed the accessibility of computers for non-expert people. Where previous systems required users to know an elaborate system of codes to work with their documents, the GUI allows anyone who can master the mouse to produce sophisticated digital work. It took until the release of the Microsoft Windows operating system in 1995 for the majority of computers to catch up to Macintosh's innovation in this area, but the easy activation of stored programs by clicking on pictorial representations of what they do (icons) has insured that the GUI is now the standard.

Another noteworthy feature of the GUI is referred to as WYSIWUG (what you see is what you get). This simply implies that what you see on the computer screen is what will be printed. This may seem like a fairly unremarkable feature in the contemporary context, but this innovation contributed to accessibility. The ability to highlight a portion of text and change its font, size, or numerous other characteristics then instantly see what it looks like makes the experience of using the technology as instantly tangible as the experience of writing calligraphy. It also increases the level of abstraction from the algorithmic processes.

One might be tempted to think that older style interfaces such as the DOS operating system locate the user closer to the binary code, but again this is barely a less abstracted means of interaction. Clarifying the term 'operating system' demonstrates why, and why this abstraction is of concern.

Most simply, an operating system is a stored program that acts as a way of connecting more specialized programs to the circuitry of the computer. In interface programs that work like DOS (Disk Operating System), the user is required to know a program language and type computer commands in order to work with programs and documents. The GUI merely replaced this process with iconic buttons that, when activated by clicking on them with the mouse, send a string of code to replace the typed command.

Though the popular movement to the GUI in computing still causes disdain among certain specialist communities of users such as hackers, it is erroneous to think that the memorization of specific file paths and execution codes locates an average user a lot closer to the binary code and logic circuits. It may eliminate the need to remember much of the language needed to operate the computer, but for the average user it doesn't necessarily limit access any more or less to the program codes that make the computer work. Those languages remain a specialized knowledge that all but the very rare computer user will even want or need to know exists — no more so than every driver wanting or needing to be an auto-mechanic.

The interface wraps the machine in a package that people can understand, making the computer a useful everyday appliance. It would be a rare individual indeed who would be able to take advantage of the technology if the machine still required its user to speak its own language. In our present generation of computers, there are several levels of languages, mnemonic in their nature (meaning a word stands in for the binary string, much as the icon in the GUI does).

Moving from the interface into the machine, the computer user steps through the main language levels as first the cultural language (the interface itself), then the program assembly language (a system of mnemonic code), followed by the interpreter or compiler (to change the programs written in mnemonic code into binary), and finally the machine language itself (the hard-wired binary circuitry). The journey outward from the code back to the user requires the same steps in reverse. Characteristics of each code system are distinct enough to call each a different language, but they all serve to reach into the circuitry of the machine and control its flows of electricity. In this way, they are all extensions of the main binary code system, and all operate according to the very same logical system. In this respect, even though it is an abstracted practice, all people who use computers are interacting with binary code. In spite of the mathematical complexities involved in the translation processes, the goal is one of practicality, minimalism, and simplicity; overall a search for the most efficient reduction to the zeros and ones of binary and back again to the cultural level. However, the cultural metaphors in computer design do not begin and end with the interface itself. Under the cover of the computer is an electronic network modeled after the physical workings of the human mind, complete with thought centers and neural network.

00100 The Computer: The hardware and the history

Though computers have evolved impressively over the past six decades to attain their present capabilities, it may be surprising to some that their fundamental design hasn't changed much since the previously mentioned EDVAC. The ability of the EDVAC design to store its programs and recall them by itself where instructed to do so guaranteed its design would be the foundation of all that followed (Campbell-Kelly & Aspray, 1996: 4, 99). Understanding the physical architecture of those 'First Generation' computers will help clarify the logic that gave rise to their possibility, and thus was embedded into them and all computers since.

Architects seek to structure human experiences in space. Similarly, the physical architecture inside of the computer structures the user's experience with the data: "architecture is ... like a conceptual paradigm, a method of organization of intellectual perspectives, opinions, or emotions" (Rockeby, 1995: 138). To understand how binary digital code came to be the dominant paradigm of information storage over the course of the 20th century, a better understanding of the technical motivations and logic that was imperative to this early equipment and its operation is necessary. Clearly, the choice of binary code as the language of electronic digital computing was seen as a purely rational and functional decision, informed by numerous historical precedents and breakthroughs in logic and engineering. However, the cultural metaphors —particularly conceptions of the mind itself— proved to be as important as abstract rational methodology in ensuring this triumph of rationalism over nature. To understand how this may be so, it is important to clarify what type of machine qualifies as a 'computer', look at some of the processes involved in the design and function of the computer, and briefly look at the popularization of the 'von Neumann' design with Boolean algebraic circuitry as the dominant electronic computer architecture.

What is a computer?

While the ENIAC (Electronic Numerical Integrator and Computer) brought into service in 1945 was what is considered an electronic digital computer; it used a 'decimal' number system, and thus was not a 'binary' computer like its successor, the EDVAC.[8] The significance of this will become clear as I explain how to differentiate between number systems, using the ENIAC and the EDVAC to illustrate why the use of 'binary' code was considered preferable for the evolution of electronic computing and information storage.

---

[8] In fact, the EDSAC (Electronic Delay Storage Automatic Calculator) was the first binary stored program computer to be completed in 1949 in England, but was based on the design of the EDVAC. It should also be noted that numerous other machines were invented that successfully performed mathematical functions, but their inability to compete with the speed of human computing teams made them more experimental curiosities than useful computational devices.

The main features that distinguish a computer from a basic calculating or adding machine include the automated programs that eliminate the need for human intervention in that process, and the ability of the computer to store its information. The computer was invented to replace people (specifically, teams of predominantly women mathematicians). To be successful, it had to be able to perform all of the functions people could do, only faster and with less chance of error. This required the invention of a quite remarkable machine; a 'universal' machine as Alan Turing called it, or a 'Turing machine' as others have described it.

Turing observed that human calculation has a linear operational process, meaning a person does only one operation at a time. The physical act of writing calculations is guided by the mentally guided program of operations needed to achieve the calculation. Corresponding to this observation, Turing envisioned the computer as comprised of both mechanical parts, which we know as hardware, and its data. A mechanical adding machine needs a person to punch in the operations. Similarly, an automated computer needs instructions describing how data should be processed. This logical stream of operations is what we know as a program. Turing worked out an ingenious system of encoding the machine's instructions alongside the data being processed, so that the program instructions appear as simply more data in the stream of information (Davis, 2000: 165). A computer, then, is a machine that is equipped to perform automatically whatever mathematical program the user selects, by storing its program as part of its data.

There have been numerous calculating machines throughout history. The desire to store numeric values temporarily to speed up the process of calculation has resulted in many ingenious inventions. For example, the pencil and paper serve to temporarily store numbers in mathematical problem solving. Perhaps the most widely known and popularly used mathematical device previous to the invention of industrial adding machines was the abacus, which was used throughout the world including the Americas prior to European contact. The abacus serves to easily demonstrate the concept of number storage to assist in mathematical operations.

There are many regional variations of the abacus, but the typical Japanese version is the most straightforward design for this demonstration (see Appendix A). The apparatus itself consists of several spindles of beads fashioned into a rack. Each bead acts as a counter. Each spindle contains four moveable beads on the bottom half of the cross bar, while each spindle on the other side of the bar (the top) has one bead. Starting at the extreme right, by sliding beads one at a time towards the cross bar the lower half of any given spindle can visually represent up to the digit '4'. The top bead may then be slid towards the middle while moving the four down to represent '5', and the increments of one may then be added again to represent up to the numeric digit '9'. A single lower bead on the next spindle to the left would then be used to represent ten, and any combination of the first spindle can be used to work through the teens. The process continues ad infinitum through the hundreds, thousands, etc.

A skilled abacus user may move the beads quite rapidly, and use the machine with a high degree of accuracy. The abacus may function as an aid in addition, subtraction, multiplication and division. In spite of its utility and popularity, the actual mathematical *process* remains in the human mind. The user moves the beads to aid their memory according to the work they are doing in their head, similar to writing the numbers on a paper as one goes. This is considered information storage. The abacus clearly demonstrates how numeric digits from zero to nine can be mechanically stored and manipulated to speed up the process of computation.

The ENIAC not only took the process of storing mathematical digits to new heights, it also fulfilled the ambition to have a machine take care of some of the mundane work necessary for long and complex computations. There had been numerous attempts to create such a machine, with varying degrees of success. By refining a system that used electrical pulses stored in vacuum tubes as the beads, and series of switches and adders (groups of switches that work as a unit) to move the information around, the ENIAC was able to process math problems faster than any machine previous.

The ENIAC was considerably faster at calculating than the many rooms full of underpaid young women employed for the purpose prior to the popularization of the electronic computer, but its architectural design was problematic for at least two reasons. First, its programs had to be set up manually, entailing a lengthy process of first designing the switch array, then setting the switches by hand. The stored program feature of the EDVAC was a vast improvement on this method, in that the various switching arrays only had to be designed once for each type of problem, and the machine itself could then automatically make the changes necessary when commanded to do so. This is what we now call software. However, this was only one way in which the architecture of the EDVAC improved on its predecessor. The second and more important innovation for this thesis was in the choice of number system used in the machine.

The base-ten (or decimal) numeric system illustrated by the abacus in Appendix A is so commonplace in Western civilization that many may never have considered the possibility of another way of counting. Non-decimal number systems have existed in numerous places at different historical times, choosing, for example, units such as thirteen or seven or nine as the most intelligent basic grouping of items. Binary number systems could be found prior to the computer in Australia and Africa (Redshaw,

1996). The South Korean flag contains a form of binary coding that references four of the eight trigrams of the *I Ching*. As a basic demonstration, where we in the tradition of popular Western thought think that ten is the point at which another digit should be added to signify counting up, in a base-seven system, the additional digit marker would be added after counting seven. The number '10' in a base-seven system would translate into eight in our decimal system.

The reasons for choosing one number system over another are usually thought to be culturally determined. For example, decimal numbers easily correspond to our ten fingers (not coincidentally also called digits). In the case of choosing the binary system over the decimal system for the computer, the cultural determinants come on a literal level from an industrial cultural logic of mechanical efficiency and mathematical rationality. A belief in one God whose glory is the infinite universe describes the overriding philosophical cultural determinant. I will deal with the literal first.

Like any other, the base-two number system works on a principle of stepping up the integers as more items are counted. The only phenomenological difference is that there are only two possible choices per grouping, represented by zero or one. For example, if there is one thing, the number will read '01', if there are two things it will read '10', and if there are three things the binary code will be '11'. The decimal number four requires an additional digit, to appear as '100'. Representing the decimal numbers zero to ten looks like this:

Decimal	Binary
0	00000
1	00001
2	00010
3	00011
4	00100
5	00101
6	00110
7	00111
8	01000
9	01001
10	01010

The binary abacus shown in Appendix B demonstrates another way to visualize the base-two system. Where the decimal abacus counts up to ten on each spindle, the binary abacus can only count one. This may at first seem like a very labour intensive way of counting, but the corresponding decimal translations above the beads show how, by doubling the signified number with every integer, counting in binary can quickly add up to very high numbers with only a short string of code. It is possible to count to thirty-one on one hand in binary by using only five fingers as markers. Binary arithmetic in fact consumes less labour and is logically simpler than the decimal system (von Neumann *et al*, 1992: 6).

Either abacus requires the user to slide the correct beads and understand the mathematical operations used. In physical labour alone, the base-two system requires moving far fewer beads. Consider the fact that the decimal-based ENIAC used approximately 19,000 vacuum tubes to store information, compared to the EDVAC's estimated 3,500 used to store even more information than its predecessor. This saving in mechanical labour alone is impressive, but when coupled with its ability to store and execute its own programs, the choice between machines in terms of efficiency is obvious.

Aside from it's labour saving advantages, it is important to understand that there is a logical reason that the binary system may be relatively easily wired into the circuitry of computers in a way that decimal system cannot. This has to do with conceptions of the human mind at various points in history by various logicians. At the time the EDVAC was being designed, the engineering logic of John von Neumann and Claude Shannon had a great impact.

von Neumann Architecture and the Mind Metaphor

In 1945 a draft document titled "First Draft of a Report on the EDVAC" began circulating among computer engineers that outlined the main details of the EDVAC computer. Through a historical accident, John von Neumann was the only name out of numerous contributors to appear on the document, and as a result, the fundamental design came to be referred to as 'von Neumann architecture'. Relatively short for its accomplishment, the document revolutionized computer design by incorporating the improvements mentioned above, but also by popularizing a certain way of thinking first proposed by Alan Turing regarding how to most successfully design a computer.

Turing claimed our astounding capacity for thought is possible because our brains are actually "universal computers," capable of performing any rational process necessary (Davis, 2000: 183). Von Neumann agreed with Turing's assessment of the human brain's enormous capacity and ability. Von Neumann's report on the EDVAC literally builds on this analogy, describing vacuum tubes as substitutes for the brain's neurons, and wiring as nerves. The report affirms that electrical circuits mimicking the human thought process in the brain are possible. The design in the report outlines the neural analogy and the basic circuit designs of each 'thought center', called "organs"; one for central control, one for addition, one for subtraction, one for multiplication etc. through all the necessary mathematical functions. Additionally, there are various sensory devices to allow interfacing, and a memory to store programs and data. The mind model implies a rather specific understanding of the human brain, but its designers also chose to ignore and also 'improve' some of what makes our minds human and not just mechanical thinking-devices.

Von Neumann *et al*'s description of the EDVAC design incorporates a description of how the relays that comprise its logical circuitry are similar to neural synapses in the human body, and that electrical pulses may act as stimuli in both cases. The "all or none" principle by which human nerves are said to trigger movement or brain activity is the key to the design. This means that when a neural synapse shoots a pulse through a nerve, it does so completely, with all of its potential force. Comparable to a bullet, there is only one powerful shot of stimulus that activates other synapses, and so on down the line until the muscle or brain activity is achieved. Equally so, electrical pulses firing through the computer circuitry work the relays without confusion.[9]

Just as pulses through the human neural net pass a stimulus through numerous axons (webs of smaller nerves), so too is computer circuitry designed to entail more than one response to a single pulse (or absence) of electricity. Even so, the authors admit the analogy doesn't necessarily entail a just representation of the actual human neural net: "we ignore the more complicated aspects of neuron functioning: Thresholds, temporal summation, relative inhibition, changes of the threshold by after-effects of stimulation beyond the synaptic delay, etc." (von Neumann *et al*, 1992: 5). In other words, the computer is really only concerned with one type of neural phenomenon —the one considered most logically

---

[9] Contemporary computers do incorporate a variety of signaling techniques to convey more information, such as variable pitches, and varying signal strength. These advances enhance the potential of the original design being discussed here, and do not entail an essentially different principle.

efficient— which the vacuum tube is said to approximate by acting as a relay and allowing current to pass (equivalent to the firing of a neural synapse) or not. This kind of simplicity is the key to the design, as the pulses representing binary numbers are processed bit by bit, one operation at a time. One noteworthy improvement in the computer neural net over the human prototype is the removal of delays along the pathway. Some delays are built into the circuitry to synchronize the various components, but overall it is designed to operate as quickly as possible—much faster than the human brain.

The opening and closing of switches is accomplished by the use of the pulses themselves. This is known as a 'relay control circuit', in which a switch is opened or closed by the use of another electrical circuit (see Appendix C). Most simply explained, by wiring together numerous types and configurations of switches and relays, the pulses create what I call a live document of binary code that opens and closes its own switches until its program is completed. This type of document is live in the electrical use of the word, as in 'live wire'. The relay switches in the EDVAC were in fact vacuum tubes, which were given up for the transistor when it was invented, which gave way to the advent of the silicon chip. Although the technology has become microscopic and has proliferated to contain thousands of relays on a single tiny computer chip, the basic principle remains the same.

The electrical pulses that are the code at its most primary level are generated by a clock within the machine that acts as a heart of sorts, rhythmically sending out the binary information that triggers the prearranged configurations of switches. The rate at which the clock pulses is one of the components determining the speed of the machine, along with the speed at which the switches can be reset and how long it takes for a signal to pass through a wire. In this arrangement, time and information are conceptually conflated into the same thing — the electrical pulses that are binary code cannot exist without the clock, and time in the machine exists as pure information. As an aside, it is interesting to reflect for a moment on the sentiments of Innis. A concept of time is once again being used technologically to control space (albeit a much smaller space than the vast territories he was discussing, and a rate of time measurement conceptually impossible for us to imagine).

In terms of the code itself, the "First Draft" tells us that '0' represents the absence of a stimulus, while '1' represents its presence. This might at first seem to contradict what was argued earlier, that zero and one cannot simply be thought of as rival opposites. If this were the case, binary code could no longer be said to communicate monadism, but there are at least two points that support the previous argument. Since it is the machine being discussed here, a literal reading of the code is our concern at this moment. The first and most technical issue is that the relay circuitry may be wired either to be on (closed) unless the relay is charged at which point it is turned off (as in Appendix C). Conversely, it may be wired to be off (open) unless there is a charge, at which point it is turned on. The intricacies of this type of issue will become more apparent when understood through the logical circuitry developed by Claude Shannon (see Appendix D for other possible arrangements of circuitry).

The second point refuting the popular myth of binary code is that a single zero or one on its own without more code to give it context does not have much depth of meaning in the working of a computer. Literally meaningful opening and closing of relay switches is accomplished through the grouping of bits into bytes, and ultimately binary 'words' that convey enough information to signify characters (Marshall, 2002). The letter 'a' standing on its own only imparts what information one subjectively infers from its presence. Likewise, a single digit '0' needs more information to put give it a context for meaning. Theoretically speaking, computer engineers could have easily chosen the algebraic signifiers 'x' and 'y' to represent the pulses instead of '0' and '1', or invented totally different symbols. Even more illustrative, if I mix lexicons and imagine that 'a' represents a pulse, and '1' a non-pulse, it would be difficult to believe that there was a hierarchy involved in binary language.

The point is that hierarchical thinking about binary code is a circumstantial subjective inference, not a characteristic of what the sign is intended to signify. In other words, the reader is imparting their own value bias into the numbers zero and one, and not necessarily interpreting them the way they are actually read by the machine. This subjective dualist inference is on a literal level disrupted by the monism of the way the code actually signifies. At the level of the user interface, zero and one do not *stay* zero and one. The pixels in the screen change with regularity, displaying new data as continuously as the program generates it or the user desires. Notation in electronic text is not a process of writing in the margins, but rewriting the code itself. The 'original' text is very literally mutated, relegating 'authenticity' to the emotional domain of nostalgia.

In the tradition of western mathematics, zero acts primarily as a place-holder, not as a value in and of itself. Thinking back to the binary abacus in Appendix B, the '0' means that there is no bead moved over — referring to Latour's concept of embedded values meant to limit the uses of our machines, the command to the user then is "don't move it—leave it where it is". Conceptually, this is no less a command than "move it." Imagine the decimal number one hundred without the zeros: 1_ _. The places that zeros are meant to appear have no values because it is one grouping made of one hundred items, but for ease of distinguishing what decimal grouping the one represents, we use the zeros to hold the one in its place. This is an important technical concept to keep in mind in considering binary code shooting throughout the machine at unimaginable speeds. The synchronization of the machine and its operating language is accomplished by the rhythmic regulation of pulses. Similar to binary code, Morse code is an intelligent codification of language because it is primarily rhythmic (i.e. uses time to mediate intelligent communication, like the rhythmic component of music). Understanding this is important in order to clarify that binary code is always active, even when there is no pulse.

The EDVAC used strings of code thirty digits long (von Neumann *et al*, 1992: 11). Binary digits (called bits) are grouped together to form bytes (usually eight bits in length), and the size of the byte determines how much detail the code will contain. In binary code, a word is the representation of a single value, which can be one byte in length, or two or more, depending on the type of computer and its circuitry. The EDVAC thus used a word that was one byte of thirty bits. Thirty bits looks like this (grouped by five's to assist in counting):

00000 00000 00000 00000 00000 00001

A word may be either a numeric value or an instruction set. The numeric value in the above binary word is one. Instructions consist of two parts: operation codes (opcode) that tell the computer to what organ it must send the information (the subtractor, divider, square rooter etc.), and addresses where the resulting number of the operation may be stored (Hayes, 1988: 22). These are conveyed by placing values on the left-hand side that distinguish what type of word it is (von Neumann *et al*, 1992: 15). For example, a one in a specific position means it is a negative number, or in a different position on the left, signifies a decimal point should be inserted in the value in a specific place. Instruction sets include commands for dealing with the information immediately implicated in the operation, and the memory address and instruction to retrieve the next instruction set. This method of writing command codes alongside data codes was first conceived by the aforementioned legendary WWII code-breaker Alan Turing, whose contribution to the technology is considered no less important than the von Neumann architecture.

There are three categorical levels involved in computer designs, each of which builds upon its predecessor to build a complex text (Hayes, 1988: 91). At the 'gate' level, the components operated by the bits of code are the switches. Next is the register level, in which binary words act on memory registers and some of the basic circuitry. Finally, blocks of words act on the processor of the computer. At that point the interface comes into play to make the processes humanly intelligible, which is an issue of software, not hardware.

The code string being as such, a meaningful binary code that performs even a simple useful operation will necessarily be quite long, and it becomes clear why trillions of calculations per second are needed in order to produce intricate works such as weather maps. Describing the fundamentals of the circuitry demonstrates just how dynamic of a text binary code is, but also how redundant.

00101 The Logic of the Circuitry

Claude Shannon's 1938 thesis, "A Symbolic Analysis of Relay and Switching Circuits," demonstrated how to build logic circuits from relay switches. His work was based in part on a treatise published in 1854 by the mathematician George Boole entitled *An Investigation of the Laws of Thought*, which he encountered as the student of American logician Charles Sanders Pierce.[10] Shannon's knowledge of relay switches and electrical engineering working under the supervision of Vannevar Bush inspired the second part of his work. Here I will show how Shannon applied Boole's themes in a very practical sense to design the reasoning machine that was fully realized in the EDVAC.

The main idea that Shannon picked up from Boole was that all human rational processes could be reduced to the three operative descriptors (now called Boolean Operators) 'and', 'or' and 'not'. Boole argued that our rational processes depend primarily of grouping together things by, for example, saying 'this

---

[10] Pierce is said to have been the first to design logic circuits based on Boole's work, but he didn't have the applied electrical knowledge needed to manifest his designs. See
<http://www.kerryr.net/pioneers/boole.htm>.

thing *and* that thing'. Similarly, we make decisions based on 'this thing *or* that thing', and to make more specific selections, we say 'this thing *not* that thing'. This model of thought conceives of a pool of all possible choices, from which specific categories of things are chosen. For example, a child may choose all the candies with the descriptor 'red' from a bowl of assorted coloured candy mixed with chocolates. In this case, the rational process includes the descriptions 'candy' and 'red'. By bringing together these two descriptors, only red candies may be selected from the container. If the child wants more than just red candy, they may choose the categories 'candy' and 'red' or 'orange', thus describing all the possible candies in the bowl they want. Conversely, if they don't want a specific kind of candy, but want all the rest, they may choose, for example, 'candy' not 'green'. This will give them everything in the bowl that is classified non-green candy. This distinction is important, because there is also something described as 'chocolate' in the bowl, which will also be excluded by default from their description, since it is a different category of thing.

This very basic description of how Boolean categorization works is meant to describe the workings within a closed environment, meaning the possible choices are limited by what is contained in the bowl. It should be noted here that Boole and Leibniz (on whose premises Boole built his philosophy) were concerned with universals, not closed sources of information. This means they would have considered it necessary to specify which bowl of candy was being searched as a category on its own, or it would be taken that all candy in the infinite universe was being searched through. Shannon was not concerned with the philosophical issues raised by tangible things, instead focusing his energies entirely on abstract mathematical values.

Kurt Godel had shown previously how, by assigning a whole number to each signifier comprising a numerical concept, all numeric values (for example, negative numbers) and mathematical operation signs (such as a '+' or '÷' sign) could be converted to 'natural' numbers (or digital integers) (Davis, 2000: 116-117). His proposition was to assign a whole number to represent each symbol, thereby allowing all mathematical operations to be written as strings of numeric code. Turing developed this idea to create the 'Turing machine'. Turing believed he had observed that when performing a calculation, a human being methodically performs one task at a time. Individual instructions could be given codes the same way the numbers and operations could be coded. A string of code could be produced in real numbers that describe in sequence how to work with the desired data (Davis: 152-159). Turing even theoretically showed how to make this code in binary form, which is how it was done in the EDVAC.

Godel's and Turing's ideas theoretically mean that, when combined with Boolean operations, all human thought processes can be represented by a series of gates reflecting the above operations. Of course, this assumes that Boole's postulates are accepted as the truth about human thought. I will not argue with Boole here, but rather move on with the understanding that his is the mathematically expressed logic by which our dominating information storage medium operates, and investigate further Shannon's application of his work to electrical engineering.

The main mechanical function Shannon was concerned with was representing the 'and', 'or' and 'not' functions of Boolean algebra in terms of electrical circuitry. This was accomplished by configuring relay switches to pass current or not according to what kind of signals were input. For example, a simple 'and' switch requires a charge on both of its inputs to output a charge. If only one or the other input (or neither) receives a stimulus, the relay will not forward a signal to the next level of relays (see Appendix D). An 'or' switch requires a stimulus on either of its inputs, but not both, to output a signal. Finally, a 'not' switch will output a signal only if nothing is input. Though several other configurations of switches are possible, combinations of these basic three configurations into 'adders' can actually represent all possible outcomes that might be desired for the function of the machine.

Creating adders out of the above relays —or 'gates' as they are also called— allows the design of a machine that is capable of any mathematical function. For example, Appendix E illustrates an addition circuit, demonstrating the equation '1 + 1'. Since the sum of the equation performed is two, there must be provision to carry the one to the next binary digit place. In this case, the carried digit will act as a signal stimulus for the next half-adder. A full-adder contains half-adders, and is designed to accept a bit carried forward from a previous calculation, itself outputting a sum and a value to carry to the next adder (see Appendix F). As one might observe, the number of switches needed to build the types of circuits that perform complex calculations, such as square roots, proliferates quite rapidly. Nevertheless, history has proven the expression of Boolean algebra through electronic relays, and powered by binary coded electrical pulses, creates an efficient computing machine.

Shannon's engineering and theoretical work went far beyond designing Boolean switching arrays. Directly related to his engineering work was his invention of digitization. Shannon's idea of sampling information from a given source at a stable rate and converting that information into a "bit stream" of binary code that could be processed by the computer is the basis of the digital revolution (Calderbank & Sloane, 2001).

Every photo that is scanned, every voice that is digitally recorded, or any other type of computer-mediated information is either originated as or converted into a "bit-stream" — the string of electrical pulses that are the binary text. Shannon devoted much of his efforts to maximizing the accuracy and message carrying potential of digital circuitry, founding the field of Information Theory with his co-author Warren Weaver. Their book *The Mathematical Theory of Communication* in 1949 outlined what would quickly become important theoretical issues in communication, not just technically, but also socially.

Perhaps best known in the social sciences for designing the 'transmissive model' of communication, Weaver and Shannon were interested only in the direct effects of communication. They defined communication as "all the procedures by which one mind may affect another" (Shannon & Weaver, 1978: 3-4), and were very aware of the arbitrariness of their decision to focus only on encoding, transmission, and decoding. Their 1949 work was concerned only with the accuracy of transmission, trying to make the received message resemble the sent message as accurately as possible. In so doing, they were careful to point out that they were working at the level of *information*, not at the level of *meaning* (ibid. 8), which requires interpretation of the sent and received information. Meaning is culturally influenced, and Shannon and Weaver were really only concerned with making a better functioning machine. Still, their work suggests a number of interesting social effects that bear some examination.

What immediately strikes a social chord in Weaver and Shannon's work is their use of the terms 'freedom' and 'nature'. In their view, the greater the range of possibility the receiver has in interpreting whatever information is sent, the greater is their freedom. The information itself is defined as "naturally" being the "logarithm of the number of choices" (ibid. 9-10). In these very technocratic postulations, freedom is something that needs to be curtailed as much as possible to facilitate more accurate transmission of information and the information is, naturally, mathematical.

What Weaver and Shannon call "probability" and "entropy" limit freedom in language (ibid. 11). The measurable degree of probable interpretations is a measure of the entropy, or redundancy, of the language used. Freedom is at its highest when all probable interpretations are equally likely to occur, meaning that freedom increases with a greater number of interpretive choices (ibid. 15-16). Fifty percent real freedom in a message means that we can choose half the words we use from our stock of memorized descriptors, while the remaining fifty percent are necessary to act as a template (ibid. 13-14). This sentence would not be intelligible without at least half of the words you are reading providing a structure for the other fifty percent to convey another level of meaning within.

While fifty percent is approximately the entropy of the English language, there is a higher degree of entropy in binary code. The circuitry of the machine acts to limit the freedom of binary messages because the only variables are the bits themselves. The spaces between pulses are a form of entropy, and the limited number of circuit relay designs act to limit probable interpretations. The rate of the internal clock, and the efficient exclusion of unwanted 'noise' in the signal also contribute to the entropy of the code. Translation into other languages (which is quite necessary with computers) and the fact that a discrete code has only two choices per bit also severely limit interpretive choices within computers, adding to entropy. A high degree of redundancy in the text helps increase the effectiveness of the transmission, by excluding other interpretive choices — single bit of information comes surrounded by one or more words of redundant information. However, even with their very technical description of communication, Shannon and Weaver, like their cohorts, believed that the binary number system conveyed a completely human message.

Adorno and Horkheimer asserted rationalists in general looked for justification in irrational foundations. Shannon and Weaver ultimately rest their rational arguments on the non-rational foundation of human intuition. In addition to the logical arguments that the base-two number system is efficient for mathematical engineering, Shannon further justifies it as preferable to base-ten because, "It is nearer to our intuitive feeling as to the proper measure" (ibid. 32). Indeed, it may also intuitively seem absurd to us that such brilliant engineering rationalism may be justified in the end by this irrational explanation. However, Boole and Leibniz demonstrate that there is a sophisticated philosophy behind Shannon's intuition.

00110 Boole's Rational Mind

The numeric digit zero conveys no literal meaning within the circuitry of the computer, acting primarily as a place-holder to space out electronic pulses to the desired time length. This is strictly a literal reading of the code, the way the machine reads it. However, the connoted meaning of the text tells us something different. In tracing it back to its source, binary code as born out of Boolean algebra appears to be a rhetorical language indeed, intended to demonstrate (or 'prove' in the mathematical sense) that Boole's propositions regarding human thought were correct. In its present form, embedded in the computer and perpetuated globally in the form of computer science and programming education, there is not much room for argument with the assumptions of the text. However, prior to its appropriation by computer engineers, the logic of Boole was most certainly open to debate.

Although one might be inclined to argue with Boole's rational, his work was pivotal in the field of logic for marrying it with mathematics (Davis, 2000: 40). His treatise was the fulfillment of Leibniz's aspiration in mathematics, providing a "calculus ratiocinator" (or 'symbolic logic') that supposedly could rationally explain the infinite universe. The contradiction involved in trying to explain the infinite hardly needs pointing out, but nonetheless that was the task Leibniz and Boole and many others set out to do. In hindsight, perhaps a more forgiving characterization of their work in practice would simply say that they were concerned with how truth claims can be rationally justified.

It is unlikely that Boole was more than fleetingly if at all aware of Leibniz's ideas (ibid. 39), but his work is tied to Leibniz's precedent in several ways. Boole's conclusion that '$x\,x = x$', the crux of binary logic, was actually proposed centuries earlier by Leibniz in the form of '$A \oplus A = A$'. This equation expresses that a given thing is not any greater than any one of its parts, nor can any one of its parts be greater than the rest. Even with this direct correlation in work, the most direct social connection between Boole and Leibniz is the unlikely intermediary Samuel Clarke.

A contemporary of Leibniz, Clarke had corresponded with him for some time in defense of a Newtonian exposition of time and space. A sticking point between the two arose from Leibniz's insistence that Clarke's elaborate argument proving the existence of God could be reduced to simple mathematical expressions, though he was not successful in proving it. Centuries later, George Boole demonstrated the effectiveness of his own calculus by (unknowingly) proving Leibniz correct (ibid. 22).

Boole's work also corresponded with Leibniz conceptually in terms of binary notation. Although Leibniz recognized the potential breakthrough in expressing any given value with binary digits, he was not successful in developing binary notation into a complete system of logic. Again, where he failed, Boole found success.

As the circuitry of the computer illustrates, Boole unknowingly contributed to the technical workings of the machine in at least two important ways. By demonstrating an algebra of logic that reduces all values to the numerals zero or one, Boole provided the theory that allows the machine to use the 'all or nothing' pulses of electricity as code. His second obvious contribution was the reduction of human thought to the mathematical operations that we now call Boolean Operators.

Boole's treatise begins with the affirmation that it is his purpose to distinguish the fundamental laws of thought, express those laws symbolically in the form of calculus, and in so doing construct the scientific method by which will be exposed the truth about the human mind and how it works (Boole, 1958: 1). Given that this premise of symbolically expressing the laws of the mind's rational processes was applied in the logical concept of the computer, it may then seem like less of a coincidence that the perceived neurological workings of the mind served as the model for the computer's physical development. Identifying Aristotle as the founder of metaphysical inquiry, Boole proposes to prove it is possible to scientifically describe the human intellect through which the laws of the operations of the mind can be discovered (ibid. 3). Working as a true positivist, Boole insisted that such laws could be found only by deep, rigorous rational investigation and reasoning. This means looking for "relations among things and relations among propositions" (ibid. 7), in contrast to the idea of looking for relations among facts. As results of rational inquiry, 'facts' are dependent on a network of justifications, making them different from 'things' and 'propositions', which stand on their own. This is because, like his predecessor Leibniz, Boole wanted to identify the *processes* of logic, and not the supposed 'facts' that this logic produces. This proposition is supposed to ensure that the method of his inquiry reflects its results and vice versa; as any good theory, it must withstand its own test. By identifying what he considered the processes of logic, Boole was developing a system by which any question could be reduced to a formulaic calculation. Any inquiry could then be settled by assigning the correct symbolic values to the idea under question, and calculating the outcome the way Leibniz had envisioned and how the modern computer actually does.

Boole was neither an engineer nor a mechanical tinker. Rather, he was every bit a mathematician and logician, and concerned with scholastic pursuits rather than designing machinery. In fact, he is the only historical figure of note mentioned in this thesis who seems not to have been concerned with building some sort of 'thinking machine'. Even so, his language of logic lends itself conceptually and practically to the computer. The practical application of Boole's theory by Shannon may lend its outcomes the appearance of profound truth, but Boole was clear in his writing that the data he is working with are arbitrarily determined.

Boole describes data in his work as comprising either something that *has* happened, or something that is *likely* to happen (ibid. 14). Expressed differently, data reflect something that already is, or probably is or will be. These things may either stand on their own as a "simple" event, or they may be "compound", meaning they are dependent on a context constructed of simple events for meaning. The example he gives is to state "it rains" as a simple event, while "it rains and thunders" is a complex event made of two simple events (ibid. 14). The point being made is twofold: first, compound events can be understood as fundamentally describable by simple events. Referring to the example of candies in a bowl, 'candy' is a simple descriptor, as is the descriptor 'red'. The combination of the two gives us the compound 'red candy'. However, we know that there is more than just red candy in the bowl (and in the universe at large), and this leads us to Boole's second point regarding simple and compound events.

Boole expresses the fallibility of data as a stable 'truth' in his description of the criteria for simple events, which are the definers of compound things: "The criterion of simple events is not ... any supposed simplicity in their nature. It is founded solely on the mode of their expression in language or conception in thought" (ibid. 14). Simple events are variable, because they may be arbitrarily chosen and expressed to define compound events, and may themselves be moved to the category of compound by describing them with other simple events. For example, the choice not to use the descriptor 'bowl' does not mean that it is not important to the event 'candy', but rather its absence betrays an assumed thought regarding the location of the candy in question. It is easy to see how an infinite regress may occur if we seek to find a 'truth' in the data by exposing all possible simple events. Boole instead focuses his investigation on causal events and probable outcomes.

Compound events are explained as a combination of simple events. This proposition is expressed in terms of probability as the combination of known events given as *A, B,* and *C* indicating the (probable) occurrence of event *X* (ibid. 16). From this point forward Boole begins to introduce his series of algebraic equations that calculate the probable outcome *X* even when the data for *A, B* and *C* aren't known. He explains that this is possible by giving these constants the limiting values of zero and one (ibid. 17), meaning each variable either did or was likely to occur (one), or didn't or was unlikely to occur (zero). Of course, directly plugging in values only leads to a restatement of the original problem, which doesn't reveal anything less hypothetical. The issue then for Boole is to determine the "Calculus of Statistical Conditions" by which to quantify possible variables without ambiguity (ibid. 17-18). This leads to his postulations regarding signs.

Boole maintains that the laws of reasoning are inherent in and revealed through mathematical signs (ibid. 24). Regardless of what is signified in terms of denotation or connotation, signs are arbitrary marks with fixed interpretations, subjected to fixed laws regarding their use. They may be combined with other signs and be reinterpreted accordingly (ibid. 25). Being a logician, Boole can subjectively fix the meaning of the sign in terms of its treatment within the equations he develops, thereby creating a complete system of logic. As he described with the concepts of simple and compound events, meaning is arbitrarily decided by giving importance to some criteria over others, but the use value of the sign is constant for Boole's system. For example, for Boole it doesn't matter if I hereby call a dog a snark, as long as my reader has the cultural background to assemble a significance for snark (which, for example, you now know means dog in this instance, but only in this instance, because the meaning of snark is imported by its use in this sentence). Even if this is so, a sign does have to have a stable significance in order to fulfill its use. This stability is found in the set of connections (simple events) that comprise the concept it represents (ibid. 26). For example, some stable connections comprising 'dog' are 'hairy', 'teeth', 'barks', 'sniffs' etc. This rendering of the sign dog makes the sign obey the laws that govern conceptualization and logical operations in the mind.

Given the arbitrariness of the sign as he describes it, Boole proposes that any set of concepts can be expressed by selecting stand-ins from the letters *a, b, c, x, y, z etc.,* as is common in algebra. He also proposes the signs +, -, and x to represent the operations by which the mind combines concepts, and the sign = to represent identity. This is now known as a typical basic algebraic lexicon, in which one can express the above description of a dog as $x = a\,b\,c\,d$, where x = dog. Although this is similar to algebra in many ways, it also differs significantly.

In a typical algebraic reading of the 'dog' equation, it would appear that the dog is a creature comprised of the multiples of its attributes, but this is not the case in Boole's appellative logical system. Rather, each letter stands in for a particular class of things alongside other classes of things. When written together, the signs *a b c d* represent a collection of all the distinct attributes each sign

70

individually refers to, not an algebraic formula in the traditional sense. In his own words:

> if x alone stands for "white things," and y for "sheep," let $x\,y$ stand for "white sheep;" and in like manner, if z stand for "horned things," and x and y retain their previous interpretations, let $z\,x\,y$ represent "horned white sheep," i.e. that collection of things to which the name "sheep," and the descriptions "white" and "horned" are together applicable. (ibid. 29)

The "things" themselves are not the important part here, but rather the concept of collections of attributes that represent and describe is. There may be numerous ways to describe a particular thing, but the process of describing it remains the same. Since the symbols are "commutative," it doesn't matter which way they are arranged; they still signify the same identity. It is here that binary begins to come into the picture.

If $x\,y = y\,x$, the classes $x\,y$ signify exactly the same thing in the end; that is, either one alone signifies the whole class of things that are $x\,y$. In this respect, neither x nor y together convey anything quantitatively more than either sign on its own or qualitatively different. Boole thus proposes that it is logical to say $x\,y = x$ (ibid. 31). But then, since x and y mean the same thing, we can say $x\,x = x$, or $x^2 = x$. Any component of the collection may be taken to signify the collection as a whole. In linguistics, this is known as metonymy, where, for example, 'the Crown' is used to describe the government of a constitutional monarchy such as Canada. This illustrates that the concern is identifying a thing by its possession of a distinct quality, not to define it by breaking down its composition.

This may all seem quite confusing at first, but a simple demonstration can clear up some of the conceptual difficulties.

Very simply, a given thing cannot logically amount to less than the things it is said to contain in its composition. As demonstrated in the description of events, neither can the things that describe another thing be quantified as being any more or less than the thing they describe. For example, if I describe a human as a thing possessing the essential characteristics perception, thought, and feeling, and I give each thing a full value of 1, I *cannot* say $1 = 1 + 1 + 1$, because that is clearly not the case. *Nor* can I quantify this human as $1 = 1/3 + 1/3 + 1/3$, because these are indefinite qualities, and there may be more that need to be added or taken away to describe a human being. However, I *can* say $1 = a\ b\ c$, where $a\ b\ c$ represent the collection of descriptors. As astute mathematicians will know, there is only one condition under which $1 = a\ b\ c$; when $a = 1$, $b = 1$, and $c = 1$. Thus a, b and c express no more nor less than each other, nor altogether more or less than the thing 'human' as a whole. Likewise, there are *two* conditions under which $x^2 = x$; when $x = 0$, or when $x = 1$. Thus no other values may be expressed in Boole's algebraic system of logic.

This system of appellative logic works fine until the point at which one wishes to describe something in terms of what qualities it doesn't possess, or when some descriptive components need to be kept apart from each other. At this point Boole's 'operators' — the same ones physically manifested in the form of relay switches— are gainfully employed.

Boole's next class of signs describes the operations by which things are aggregated into a whole, or by which a whole thing is separated into its constituent parts. Aggregate signs bring together descriptors that need to remain distinct from each other, using the concepts of 'and' and 'or', which are both expressed with the sign '+'. For example, horses and dogs, though they contain many similar attributes, must remain conceptually distinct from one another. This being the case, conjunctions can be used to keep concepts distinct. Thus, horses as x and dogs being y may be expressed as $x + y = y + x$. To add a third distinction such as brown represented by z to both categories (such as in the appellative system described above), we end up with the equation $z (x + y) = zx + zy$. The quality brown is ascribed equally to the distinct concepts of horse and dog. This means that appellative description may be added to aggregate concepts by applying it fully to all aggregate parts. This is the case not only when conjoining things, but also when excepting things.

Exceptional signs are represented with a minus sign to distinguish the separation of things with a particular quality from the remaining group. For example, I may wish to distinguish all dogs (x) except hounds (y), which may expressed as $x - y = -y + x$. I may then wish to ascribe the descriptor brown (z) to the formula, in which case I end up with $z (x - y) = zx - zy$. Here I am describing all brown dogs with the exception of brown hounds, demonstrating the ascriptive property described above. To this point there are not yet any causal or deductive propositions in this algebra, but rather simply ways of restating the same thing, even in the case of appellative signs.

Propositional sentences entail a sense of being, represented by the '=' sign. Thus far, only mundane observations such as 'horses and dogs *are* dogs and horses' have been affirmed. Boole moves into a more sophisticated realm of deduction by proposing, "The stars [x] are the suns [y] and the planets [z]" (ibid. 35). This is expressed in the equation $x = y + z$. One can infer from this that, with the planets removed, the remaining stars are suns: $x - z = y$. This ability to transpose a term from one side to the other is in keeping with standard algebra, but, due to the affirmation that all qualities are in and of themselves whole, the transposition of terms in the traditional algebraic form ends here:

it cannot be inferred from the equation

$$zx = zy$$

that the equation
$$x = y$$
is also true. (ibid. 36)

Recall that it may well be that brown (z) horses (x) are equal conceptually to brown (z) dogs (y), hinging on the common concept that they are brown (which is not designated an aggregate quality), but it definitely is not the case that horses are dogs (which are designated aggregates).

To this point, we have a system of logic that uses basic algebraic expressions, and which is limited to the integers zero and one. Boole considers the method within these limits to be the "Algebra of Logic," in which the symbols in question are divided only by arbitrarily decided differences of interpretation (ibid. 37-38). Operations of the mind ultimately rest on their interpretation in language: "The operation which we really perform is one of *selection according to a prescribed principle or idea*" (ibid. 42-43). The basic function of the mind is to select descriptions based on a method which is embedded in the way language works, like a computer search tool looks for assigned descriptors in a database. Regardless of the subject, the system of selection of descriptors and subsequent identification of concepts remains the same. Boole asserts that those processes are in fact mathematical in their nature, and that they form the "essential laws of human language" (ibid. 45). Having thus established that the operations in his system of logic are rooted in language, Boole goes on to explain the logical significance of zero and one.

The class of things represented by zero is called "Nothing," while one is considered the class "Universe" (ibid. 47). These are the two limits to all things. Since the integers are the measure of the presence of a quality and not the tabulation of things possessing the quality, zero and one sufficiently indicate the absence or presence of the class in question.

While "nothing" is the straightforward understanding that there is nothing at all in possession of the given descriptive class, the term "universe" is explained as indicating *all* things in existence characterized by the class (ibid. 48). This gives Boole the opportunity to express the things *not* in a given class as the exclusion of that class from the universe of choices. For example, if 1 signifies all dogs in the universe, $1 - x$ signifies all things not dogs. Given this equation, as per Aristotle's principle of non-contradiction, it is impossible for something to both possess and not possess a given quality at the same time. This impossibility is expressed as the formula $x (1 - x)$, which will result in zero, regardless whether $x = 1$ or $x = 0$.

I have shown how Boole demonstrated the notion that human thought occurs on the level of secondary —or "abstract"— signification. That is, while symbolic validity is not dependent on algebraic interpretation, logical validity very much is. In the process he demonstrated analysis and classification as a dichotomous process. His method results in the division of things into opposing pairs for distinction from one another, which he calls the "law of duality" (ibid. 51). This sounds problematic for the position argued at the beginning of this thesis, but Boole's 'duality' is not the same as Cartesian 'mind/body' dualism which splits a thing into its attributes. Boole is not proposing that a thing can be anything other than what it is, otherwise it ceases to be that thing. Descriptors such as 'mind' and 'body' may go towards a description of 'person', but person stands as a class on its own without division between these categorical qualities, just as a shirt is a shirt whether it is green or red or any other colour. Fixation on descriptors leads to infinite regress, not a truth statement. Expressed digitally, the sum is 1 and the person described exists, or the sum is 0 and a 'person' with those qualities doesn't exist. It can't be any other way, since the subtle variability of analog plays no part in Boole's model of human thought. The thought process for Boole is simply a matter of plugging arbitrary classes (or properties) into the logical formulas for deduction, in order to discern whether a given proposition 'is' or 'is not'.

Out of the system of basic, or 'primary', logical statements above, Boole demonstrates how to express more complex propositions. He uses the example of wealth (w) as possessing the qualities "things transferable" (t), "limited in supply" (s), "productive of pleasure" (p), or "preventative of pain" (r) (ibid. 59). Because the 'or' operator entails a selection between p or r, when taken together they may be expressed as $p + (1 - p) r$. He shows the entire sentence, "wealth is transferable, limited in supply, productive or pleasure or preventative of pain" may be expressed in the algebra of logic as $w = s\,t\,\{p + r\,(1 - p)\}$.

Boole describes several more types of propositional formulas, but he is clear in pointing out that these calculations do not define, but rather bring together classes of description (ibid. 62). While the significance of the data is subject to interpretation (or definition in that regard), the symbolic validity of the process is not open to debate (ibid. 68). Every constituent of the formulas in question must meet a strict set of criteria, ensuring the process is consistent in all cases it is applied. This bringing together of classes is the fundamental technical function of logical circuitry in computers, accomplished through the binary algebraic system of Boole. This being so, I will now examine some of the more social aspects of his work, and work through some of his underlying assumptions.

Boole's Assumptions and Monistic Conclusion

Given the thorough positivism throughout his work, what is perhaps most interesting about Boole's final chapter in *The Laws of Thought* is his turn in the end to cultural authority and ultimately faith. In spite of his certainty that his methodology is a reflection of the way we think, Boole admits that this method is in

76

practice fallible. In spite of his demonstration of the law of duality, he maintains that if we follow the complex interconnections of all things, all must be reconciled as one in the end. Running throughout is a recognition of the profound subjectivity that every human may be said to possess.

Boole's discussion of "The Constitution of the Intellect" begins with the affirmation that humans are naturally moral. Everywhere humans are observed, morality is in play. In other words, cultural values are evident everywhere in society. This morality is a product of the intellect, which is a "debatable and speculative territory" (ibid. 400). Because of this, he finds it prudent to clarify some of his more contentious conclusions. The over-arching issue Boole feels he needs to clarify is his reconciliation of dualism.

Having demonstrated his method by dividing things into two levels of order, such as simple and compound events, primary/concrete and secondary/abstract signification, nothing and universal sums, Boole asserts that distinct as these categories may be from one another, they are in fact coexistent. Rather than being completely separate, he considers these qualities "blended" ingredients within the context of his algebra of logic (ibid. 414). He insists that it is human nature to seek order, and that there is a profound 'Order' to the universe. It is this 'Order' that connects all things conceptually in one manner or another, with a profundity that is impossible for humans to imagine in its entirety. For this reason, the best people can ever conclude from their investigations is "probable" or "approximate" truth (ibid. 403). Still, he maintains that every truth is connected to others in such a way as to reveal something about the "primal unity" of the "one eternal Truth" (ibid. 415).

Though we can only approximate truths, abstract inquiry is still a necessary part of being human; Boole maintains that it is human's nature to seek answers. However, sounding like a postmodernist, he tells us that we learn more about our preconceived notions of a thing than we do about the truth of the matter:

> if the process of reasoning be carefully analyzed, it will appear that abstraction is made of all peculiarities of the individual to which the conclusion refers, and the attention confined to those properties by which its membership of the class is defined. (ibid. 404)

He argues that whether discussing observed or experienced facts, or rationalist 'necessary truths' born in thought alone, the universe is infinite, and thus neither method of understanding can be said to satisfy a full understanding of anything. Nor can it be proven in any way that one begat the other (ibid. 405-406, 418). The only reasonable approach for Boole is to seek reconciliation between materialism and idealism by acknowledging their relationship with one another. The 'real' is the observable by which abstract concepts can be postulated and thus theorized, while theory helps direct our gaze rationally to a positivist methodology. The need for Boole to philosophize in this manner becomes apparent when the paradox he himself presents to us is considered.

In mathematics, a paradox is the same as an error. Boole commits a rational error quite early on by stating that '0' is a denial, and remaining constituents in the equation are the classes of things that constitute the universe. The issue may at first sound merely semantic, but by his own method he cannot say that zero doesn't exist, especially when he himself is using it as a class in his equations.[11] The issue is simple. There cannot conceptually *not be*

---

[11] It is highly unlikely that I am the first person to take Boole to task for his paradoxical proposition, but affirm at the same time that this flaw in his logic presented itself upon applying his own method to his work (as he suggests early on should be the case).

something that is already conceived of. This is especially so since, by Boole's definition, *all* things are arbitrary classes, and '0' is literally assigned the class of nothing (ibid. 47). The class 'nothing' is quite obviously conceived of, delineating something that is not supposed to be. He is saying the universe (x) is everything (y) and nothing else (z): $x = y\,z$. This formula must be appellative, not an aggregate, because it would be inadmissible to add anything to what is already conceived as 'everything'. Because we know it *is*, the universe has to be '1', and thus in order to obtain, z must be '1' in this equation, not '0'. 'Nothing' as conceived and used by Boole must be part of the universe — nothing describes the universe as much as everything does. In the terms he proposes, $0 = 1$, which is, of course, absurd. This problem cannot be avoided by leaving out the issue of 'nothing else', because there is then no way to distinguish the universe (another problematic proposal, but I will not take this second paradox up at this time). Errors must make up part of the universe, otherwise errors could not be said to happen.

Even without the above provocation, Boole freely acknowledges the large role error plays in the universe: "The mathematical laws of reasoning are, properly speaking, the laws of *right* reasoning only, and their actual transgression is a perpetually recurring phenomenon" (ibid. 408). Seemingly oblivious to the crash in his own system revealed by his own method, he attributes error in the universe to a competition between various laws, in which they may interfere with each other. Rather than see this as chaotic, Boole suggests this is part of a grander natural order, and that it only goes to prove the fallibility of the intellect (ibid. 417).

Flawed as it may be, embedded in the circuitry of our computers, Boole's logic is the logical knowledge storage and retrieval system in which we put our faith in this digital society. There are some distinctions that should be acknowledged, such as the fact that the universe for the computer's logical system is in fact easily demarcated as the data contained in the various storage devices available to the machine. Even the potentially vast amount of data linking databases throughout the world via the internet entails a closed environment, not the infinite expanse of the real universe as Boole discusses. In as much as we rely on computers for information, our universe is limited to that which has been digitized and is accessible to the machine we are using.

Additionally, the subjectivity of the inputter and the user are both generally acknowledged. In the computer, the prescription of classes is done by whoever enters the data, subjectively deeming some descriptors important and others not. Likewise, data retrieval is dependent on the user correctly understanding the operators and classes of things available in constructing a search. Boole's logic is most visibly demonstrated when conducting internet searches with a search tool, but also the fallibility of the machine is well known to regular users. A misplaced spacebar or return button keystroke can easily interfere with the operation of the machine, and code garbled by routine malfunctions regularly cause computers to crash. In these cases, it is difficult for us to accept Boole's argument that there is a competition among laws of the universe causing such errors. It seems more fitting to affirm that there may be some theoretical problems with the code itself, or mechanical error, or perhaps both.

Flaws and errors aside, it has been the intention of this thesis to expose the cultural values —as it turns out, monist rules of thought and reason— that binary code conveys. In Boolean algebra, monism is assumed over dualism, although the monism he proposed as a reconciliation of the real/ideal schism is prone to infinite regress if we look for truth only in results of causal relations. Instead, truth is a stable pattern of processes by which concepts can be said to link to each other. Although ultimately the 'Truth' is unknowable to us as humans, it nonetheless does exist, and one may see glimpses of parts of it by positivist methods. There is some significant correlation between the work of Boole and Leibniz regarding algebraic processes, and the monist philosophical orientations of both make a look at Leibniz —one of the inventors of the algebra used by Boole— essential for a well-rounded understanding of the philosophy behind binary code.

00111 Leibniz's Inventions

Leibniz made at least four important contributions to the development of computing, including initiating formal logic as a field of inquiry, recognizing calculation could be automated, inventing a digital mechanical calculator of his own, and finally, the notion that it is possible to test hypotheses with a machine (Goldstine, 1993: 9). As distilled from Boole's work, the logic of the computer circuitry is rationalist monism, and it is of no small importance that Leibniz, another monist, is identified with the logical foundation of the computer.[12]

Leibniz worked throughout his life in pursuit of an idea he had in his youth inspired by Aristotle's method of conceptual categorizations. Leibniz thought that by creating an alphabet to represent concepts, sentences could be formulated that would reveal the nature of the relationships between categories, and thereby test the validity of given statements. While he did make some progress towards this goal, it wasn't until Boole that such a complete logical language was worked out. However, where Boole

[12] This is not to dismiss lightly the contributions of numerous other important figures in the evolution of calculus and logic, such as Galileo, Descartes, Pascal, and Newton among others.

was not necessarily interested in making a machine to perform his calculations, this was every bit a part of Leibniz's vision. He compared rational logic to a mechanical process, leading him to ultimately think of reason as something a machine could do more accurately and efficiently than people (Davis, 2000: 8). Leibniz thought relegating reasoning to machines would result in greater freedom for humanity:

> the astronomers surely will not have to continue to exercise the patience which is required for computation. It is this that deters them from computing or correcting tables, from the construction of Ephemerides, from working on hypotheses, and from discussions of observations with each other. For it is unworthy of excellent men to lose hours like slaves in the labor of calculation which could safely be relegated to anyone else if machines were used. (in Goldstine, 1993: 8)[13]

Towards this goal, he invented a machine incorporating what is known as the "Leibniz wheel" that could add, subtract, multiply and divide. This very popular legacy of his lived on in the form of adding machines even into the late twentieth century, only to be replaced by another machine incorporating some of his important ideas. After Pascal, Leibniz is widely recognized as the historical origin of our contemporary concept of mechanized —or machine-calculated— thought.

Leibniz's contributions to the invention of calculus were of great importance in its evolution, not the least of which was his successful invention of several symbols that represent

---

[13] Leibniz's language here reveals a great deal as regards the disdain for the work of manual calculation. Though seen unfitting for "excellent men," history shows it was apparently thought suitable for large teams of women to "lose hours like slaves" in the work of calculation.

sophisticated concepts. The pursuit of an alphabet to represent mathematical concepts led Leibniz to develop techniques that were relatively easy to use in comparison to his contemporary rival, Isaac Newton, and thus many of his ideas live on today. Though his famous rivalry with Newton over who was the first to invent calculus was of some concern,[14] Leibniz's real passion continued to be the development of the symbolic alphabet that he envisioned encompassing all of human thought, and the rules for its proper use. Along the way, he discovered binary notation, which, even though he considered it the proper notation to expose the essence of mathematics, he failed to develop to satisfaction:

> he believed (with some justification) that he was the first person to have the idea that all the information in the universe could be coded in terms of different combinations of 1 and 0; or, in his more mystical moments, the different degrees of separation of created things from God (=1, or pure active being in its absolute simplicity) and matter (=0, or absence of being, and passivity or matter). (Ross, 1999)

Leibniz envisioned his project in three phases. The first entailed compiling the entirety of human knowledge into volumes, then secondly assigning symbols to the main ideas discerned from those volumes. The third phase would be the development of the symbolic logic —or the rules— to properly use the symbols in deductive calculations (Davis, 2000: 16). It was Boole who completed Leibniz's ambition by, at least in theory, reducing all logic to a minimal number of signs. It may seem preposterous to us in the twenty-first century that Leibniz (and Boole for that

---

[14] Numerous sources report that in fact Newton and Leibniz had both invented each their own calculus in parallel at the same time, though because of a delay in the mail Newton was led to believe Leibniz had plagiarized his work.

matter) thought everything in the universe could be reduced and explained in a single algebra of logic. It may be even more absurd for us to accept that this basic premise not only guides the workings of the digital machines we operate, but it forms the philosophical foundation of science itself. The drive to reduce the infinite universe to binary code is a historically deep-rooted mania in Western thought, but one that seemed attainable to Leibniz, Boole, and a good number of other thinkers, dare I say even in the present age. Leibniz explained philosophically why he thought this would be possible.

As I move into Leibniz's philosophy of monism, it bears pointing out once more that the appellative system of logical algebra appropriated by Boole was in fact previously developed by Leibniz. His axiom 'A $\oplus$ A = A' signified that expressing conceptual logic in algebraic terms differs from expressing a system of mathematics. For example, adding books to a library collection doesn't change the fact that a library is a singular collection of books. As demonstrated by Boole, a thing cannot logically be more or less than the sum of its parts; it is fully what it is made up of, and is equally that which it constitutes. This philosophical stand implies that every thing in the universe somehow stands on its own, yet at the same time —because descriptors are shared among distinct things— things are somehow complexly interconnected and related to one another. Being a rationalist, Leibniz assumes that above all there is a divinely rational Order to the universe, and even though humans cannot know the one infinite Truth ourselves, we can come to rationally understand the interconnections of the more specific things to which we put our minds. If this all sounds self-contradictory, perhaps it is because it ultimately rests on a version of unprovable faith in God.

Leibniz's version of monism is built around the concept of "monads." He describes monads and outlines his philosophy of their being the substance of the universe in his short 1714 essay,

"The Monadology." I turn to this work to better explain the philosophical justification for trying to reduce the universe into binary code.

Monadology: Leibniz's Monism

Leibniz describes monads as the units that comprise the essential (or his descriptor is "simple") substances of the universe.[15] Unidentifiable by human perception, they can only be rationally known, prompting George Ross to comment that they are more understandably described as "mathematical points", although they are considered "infinitely complex" (Ross, 1999). Though they are nonmaterial and have no shape nor parts, no movement nor position, monads may be distinguished from each other only by the different qualities that each one manifests. Leibniz claims the universe is comprised of the appellative assembly of monads, but because monads have nothing we as humans can use to distinguish one from the other sensationally, the universe we perceive with our senses is in fact an illusion. Like the monads that comprise it, the actual universe is without shape, movement, position and extension. However, even if we can't through our senses perceive the reality of the monads and, by extension, the universe, we all have an inherent notion of what they are because they comprise in each of us our own essential self.

Though there is no outward perception, internally monads have feeling and perception. However, unlike humans, a monad is self-contained (again, "simple") and thus nothing from outside can change it inside; it follows that one monad cannot act to cause change in another. Nor can a monad be divided further than it

---

[15] This summary of "The Monadology" is a composite distilled from several translations of Leibniz's original text, and in part paraphrasing Herbert Wildon Carr, "A General Summary of the Theory of Monads" in *The Monadology of Leibniz*, R. Latta and G. M. Duncan (trans), Los Angeles: University of Southern California, 1930.

already is, such as physical matter like atoms. This doesn't mean that they are unchanging outwardly, but rather that they are in fact a type of power or force. In every monad is the potential for the realization of anything in the universe. This vast potential for the most part lays dormant until its appetite causes it to manifest itself differently to satisfy its own desire or need. This is an act of sheer will. Because this appetite is never fully satisfied, monads are in a state of constant change, and hence there is unabating change in its perception of itself.

Though monads are each uniquely individual, a shared ideal in their constitution makes them each individually strive for the same common goal, simulating the appearance that they are somehow bound together. Leibniz explains that every human being has an example of this harmonious relationship within, since the soul is a monad and the body has its own set of monads. While both soul and body go to make up humans, they act independently of one another to satisfy their respective appetites, but in striving for a common goal, give the appearance of working together. The harmony of activity produced is ultimately the work of God, who has programmed a series of necessary happenings, or appetites, in each monad at the time of its creation, that each will thus seek to fulfill. This may be analogized as a symphony, in which individual instrumentalists each play their own composed part, but by playing at the same time, create the illusive perception of a unity of sound (Carr, 1930: 21). Likewise are constructed the things we perceive as bodies. Even so, each from its own point of view, every monad is representative of the universe as it really exists. Since time and space are illusions, the universe can only be expressed as the potential of an infinite expanse or range of monads. This sounds similar to the 'universe' inside the computer, represented by the pulses which we know as zeros and ones in binary code; each digit can seem like a monad in itself, being that each pulse is pure existence. Each electrical pulse in the computer exists independent of those it is surrounded by. By manipulating and synchronizing the pulses —by playing the part of creator— humans inscribe a program for their existence that creates for us on a human scale of perception the impression of order negotiated between pulses, which is simply not the case.

Conscious awareness of individual perceptions within each monad form a range of possibility based on clarity. The clearer the self-awareness of a monad, the more it is able to recognize itself as a distinct thing. Perception implies degrees of self-awareness. This is what distinguishes one monad from the others. Though their make-up is identical, the way they manifest themselves will be according to their individual level of clarity, and their level of clarity will be unique to each and every one. This, along with their specific motivating appetite at any given moment, constitutes their intrinsic difference from one another.

Monads might not be able to distinguish one perception from another because they may be overwhelmed by the entire collection of perceptions within. However, once clarity of one perception is attained, it is easier to attain greater clarity in others. The range of clarity is characterized as three main levels; most removed from God is obscurity and confusion, then some clarity —at which point they may be called souls— and finally, clarity of necessary truths, at which point they may be called rational souls. In this way, Leibniz shows that we can rationalize a hierarchy of monads in any living thing, most particularly in humans, in which rational souls are made manifest. This is how I can distinguish my essential self (my soul) from the electrons that stimulate my brain activity; both may be monads, but of different levels of clarity. However, all monads are immortal — there is no birth nor death, only transformation in which monads grouped as an organized body may, by their own intelligence and power, constantly change their perceptions. This constant change is analogical in the sense that it is gradual, not making any jumps from one position to another. Change is also logical in the sense that what follows is directly dependent that which preceded it. Like the first law of thermodynamics that states energy can be transformed from one form to another, but it cannot be created or destroyed, monads simply *are*. Incomprehensible God brought them into existence, and they thus always have been and always will be unless, by some divine act, God decides existence of the universe will cease.

Leibniz's monadism presumes *a priori* infinite knowledge of the universe in all things, although we will never perceive with exact clarity what that knowledge is unless we become God. It also implies a form of predestination, in that the universe we have is the only one we can have. As he puts it, out of all potential outcomes, this is the "best possible" universe (in Carr, 1930: 141), its existence caused by God *a priori*. Perhaps above all, "The Monadology" purports an extreme individualism and subjectivity. Beyond a liberal philosophical atomism in which individuals jostle with each other for position, monads only appear to be in direct relation to each other. Leibniz maintains that in reality, monads are connected to each other insofar as they all execute God's plan in what we humanly perceive as perfect harmony, each striving for its own subjective perfection in the process. However, the harmony we perceive is an approximate aesthetic, made up of countless individual existences that blur into one grand experience. This is similar to how the pixels on the computer screen trick us into believing we are having an analog visual experience. This is a rather stark proposition for society and cooperation between people. As one source of criticism puts it, "Monadism leads to solipsism, that extreme form of subjective idealism which maintains that man can know nothing but his own subjective internal mental states, without the possibility of ever knowing whether anything objective corresponds to his ideas" (The Radical Academy 2001).

Leibniz's work is premised on the two rationalist principles of metaphysical investigation: the principle of non-contradiction, and the principle of sufficient reason (Carr, 1930: 70-71). The principle of non-contradiction is much like Boole's law of duality, namely that something cannot be true and false at the same time, and if something is true, its opposite is false. The principle of sufficient reason simply maintains that something is true because there is sufficient cause for it to be so. Though we may not know the full range of reasons for it being true, we can be reassured that nothing happens by mere chance, and there is ample cause for any truth such that it would be inconceivable for it not to be thus.

Given the premises and conclusions of "The Monadology," it is perhaps more obvious now how Leibniz could propose to explain rationally the universe through symbolic logic. Since everything is linked rationally within each monad according to God's plan, and since with the proper logical tools we may bring parts of that plan into clarity, any and every problem may be solved by calculation. With no such thing as accidents, the rational connections between all things simply await rational discovery. It was Leibniz's belief that after transcribing any given problem into his symbolic language, what he called "men of good will" could then easily calculate the solution with pen and paper, the result of which would be beyond challenge (Davis, 2000: 17). Of course, this is exactly what Boole did with his algebra of logic, reducing every proposition to an algebraic test of validity, to be expressed either as being of the universe (one) or not (zero).

Leibniz's monadism is the historical inspiration of our present epistemological shift, insofar as the computer and digitization may be affecting our way of knowing the world. It is worth noting the 'postmodern' crisis we are facing theoretically perhaps not coincidentally has its precedent in the logic incorporated in the computer. The 'all things being equal' appellative constitution of concepts found in Boole's work have their precedent in the solipsistic monads of Leibniz. Irrational appeals to a divine ordinance permeate the philosophical justifications of both. The 'end of reason' in mathematics seems to have come with Bertrand Russell's exposure of a paradox in set theory, by demonstrating that sets are potentially more than just one thing (Davis, 2000: 77, 56). The impossibility of representing the infinite string of real numbers is now widely recognized. In Leibniz's terms, this would be conceptually the same as trying to count every monad that exists, which is an impossible task. Additionally, many logicians are eager to point out the fallibility of our human logical and perceptual faculties. Indeed, it is an imperfect logic that is hard-wired into our thinking machines. Even so, it is the logic we have, and we must accept that, whether we agree with Leibniz that this is the "best possible world" or not, it is indeed the world we have inherited. The compulsion to rationalize our existence in it is a curious enough social phenomenon, but the impetuous drive to represent our universe in binary code has brought us some curious puzzles and crises to sort out.

01000 Conclusion

There is something reassuring about information received from computers. It is simply there, not to be argued with, but to be either accepted as the truth or rejected. It is impossible for the computer to find meaning in what it's code says. Only we humans do that. Machines only function. This can also be reassuring. We are presented with information regarding what we are concerned with, from which we may judge what we believe to be fact or fiction. The machines perform the tasks we tell them to and report the results with an unwavering dedication; that is their only purpose. They are not motivated, but rather we are motivated to use them (even skeptics and contemporary Luddites). We use them in ways that are intelligible to us. As a society, in many ways we trust our lives to the correct functioning of computers and the strings of binary code flashing through them. We trust them to do what their inventors intended to do, including convey the messages of their creators. We execute the programs built into the technology, and in many respects welcome the results.

A recurring theme in all aspects of this investigation has been faith. Leibniz and Boole rest their rational works on a faith in God. Shannon and Weaver rest their theories of information on a faith in their version of human nature. Von Neumann *et al* put their faith in an electronic model of what they considered the natural human mind. Just as we have faith that our automobile safety devices and other machines will perform their duties to prevent our injury, we also put faith into our thinking machines to accurately calculate solutions to the problems we put to them. I have argued that by accepting the information conveyed by binary code and the use of computers, we also put faith in Leibniz's and Boole's composite description of the universe.

The digital revolution perpetuates a way of knowing that tells us we shouldn't trust the material, that the physical universe is all illusion, just as Leibniz affirmed. Far from resting their arguments on solid rational proofs, the rationalists responsible for embedding these values —these rules of reason— into binary code have passed on to us non-rational justifications for the world as we are coming to know it. Where dualists instilled in society the certainty that the physical universe can be easily contained under the dominion of our superior intellect, the monism embedded in the computer tells us that this is *all* fallible. This is not to suggest that dualism somehow provides a more reliable Truth about the universe, just that the logic behind binary code is different from dualism, and in as much as we trust computers to solve our problems, monism is influencing our world-view. The algebra of logic developed by Boole was intended to do exactly that.

The fulfillment of Leibniz's vision of reducing reason to calculation, and the building of a machine to perform those calculations, make us very data dependent. Data is the result of digitization, but data in itself is not even information. Consider:

> 1234567.89 is data.
> "Your bank balance has jumped 8087% to $1234567.89" is information.
> "Nobody owes me that much money" is knowledge.

"I'd better talk to the bank before I spend it, because of what has happened to other people" is wisdom. (Howe, 1999)

Shannon and Weaver's definition of communication is the ability of one mind to affect another, but this is not considered possible with monadism; all substances are essentially independent of one another. Monads do not communicate. Since wisdom is a social construct, monads cannot be wise. Binary code simply expresses being and, at its most sophisticated capacity, information, but not wisdom or even knowledge. The appellative system of description ensures that data organization is non-hierarchical — all descriptors are equally valid. A category may be selected from all known things based on one characteristic just as easily as another. Sub-selection is a matter of subjective inference, looking for patterns (meaning) in the data, or more precisely, looking for data that backs up one's thought. Of connotated meaning, Barthes writes, "the code of the connoted system is very likely constituted either by a universal symbolic order or by a period rhetoric, in short by a stock of *stereotypes* (1988: 18). This arbitrariness means almost any idea could be found to be supported by some piece of evidence found in a computer memory somewhere, especially in the far reaches of the internet, and if it's not, it easily could be invented and added. Rather than stabilize the cultural knowledge base, this undermines the positivist credibility of any data from which we assemble our knowledge, since credibility becomes recognized as an entirely subjective decision. This is not to argue that it wasn't so before the advent of computers, but that the philosophy and method of our present mode of information storage heightens this crisis of credibility. Since all meaning is considered arbitrary in binary logic, infinite regress is the only reward for the inquiring mind.

As Lyotard points out, knowledge in our "computerized" society is a product of semantics, arrived at through a narrative process that supercedes rationalist scientific credibility (1996: 432). What we believe is as much or more a choice of who we wish to impress as it is a matter of attaining wisdom. For example, references to God by Leibniz and Boole can be read as their felt need to impress the authorities of their times. This condition keeps us fixated at the level of data and information, guided by the wisdom that all is dependent on how well we use language to maintain our social relations. The ever-changing lexicon demands our full attention, affirming the universe we perceive is nothing but an ever-changing illusion; in Baudrillard's words, all is simulation.

Though the enormous databank we call 'cyberspace' is a dispersed (yet nonetheless physical) domain, it too appears to us to be without limit to its expanse and ability to change. The world's latest information archive is an open text, always subject to further modification and plundering. The limitless potential of information storage and retrieval by linking together databases (i.e. the 'net') is constantly being enhanced in attempts to make its information describe 'reality'. For example, aside from such projects as scanning (i.e. digitizing) the entire topographical surface of the earth and, conversely, working with micro-robotic technology (to digitize the human body internally), it is also seen as imperative to develop a database of 'common sense' for computers to rely on (Sems, 2002: 7). The point is to digitize even our everyday taken-for-granted knowledge about the way that the world is. Our most basic, routine understanding of how to survive alongside one another will also soon be subject to the logical test of the computer. This will contribute to the popular myth that computers are somehow wise, as if they will have an analytical understanding of our own idiosyncrasies that we ourselves are not aware of. However, even if they can be made to mimic wisdom, computers cannot be wise.

Digital computers cannot be analogical, which is the level of meaning. Some people may be able to fool others into believing their mechanical inventions think, but the computer is meant to be an android that replicates and aids the rational processes of the human brain. Even the most clever machine designs are human in origin, and built to fulfill human aspirations. Failed attempts to create artificial intelligence in computers have proven that human thought is more than just recalling information from a big database (for example, see Dreyfus, 1994). Intelligence and meaning require experience and interpretation, not just the assembly of data. Wisdom requires the ability to learn new experiences and processes, not just information about them. The dynamic processes that constitute binary code are redundant in the extreme. Computers do not experience new things. They simply process ever-increasing amounts of data in the same way they have for decades, only faster.

Although computers and binary code fulfill Leibniz's original vision, it is obvious that they do not nor are they ever likely to mimic all human thought processes, nor have they actually replaced our social processes of negotiation and argumentation. The domain of digital technology is limited to very specific times, places and uses in comparison with the vastness of life itself. Binary code demarcates a closed value system, meaning a system that is concerned with what goes on within the relatively stable physical parameters of digital technology, the rules of which are concerned with what Boole considered the "right" way of reasoning. When a machine reaches the limit of its ascribed code of conduct, if it fails to perform in the "right" way, it stops or is considered a malfunction, not a willful act for which anyone is responsible. Mainly, machines just keep doing what they are supposed to do. By being so strongly fixed in their programs, machines show us that we humans like to regularly step outside of cultural values and modify them to our own ends. For example, when one receives a parking ticket only one minute after the meter has run out, we obviously argue with the parking attendant, not the meter.

Whether we identify changes accompanying digital technology as good or bad, or even inconsequential, is dependent in many ways on our historical reference point. Horkheimer and Adorno put it in context:

> When a new mode of social life allowed room for a new religion and a new way of thinking, the overthrow of the old classes, tribes, and nations was usually accompanied by that of the old gods. But especially where a nation ... was brought by its own destiny to change to a new form of social life, the time-honored customs, sacred activities, and objects of worship were magically transformed into heinous crimes and phantoms. Present-day fears and idiosyncracies, derided and execrated character traits, may be deciphered as the marks of the violent onset of this or that stage of progress in human development. (Horkheimer & Adorno, 1995: 92)

In our present state of knowing, it is considered unwise by our wise ones to claim any truth as absolute. It is not possible to claim any knowledge other than one's actual lived experiences, but even then, one's memory is subject to challenge as a source of invention. Where a competition of experiential interpretations ensues, corroboration of evidence is used as a method to calculate and manufacture a truth. Power and authority impose what they deem acceptable to believe based on the technologies of calculation, persuasion and discipline. However, change does take place in spite of the will to control. As Horkheimer and Adorno point out, to understand this is so we need only to look at how that which was formerly celebrated is now that which is derided. In the case of knowledge, it is now positivism and dualism with their claims of objectivity that invite the harshest scorn of contemporary philosophy and theory. For those of us inclined to speculate and tell stories about what we think and why, to what exact degree this change in our way of knowing the world is a result of our dependence on binary code or a coincidence will ultimately remain an unsolvable calculation. The story will remain an open text. However, we can have faith that even if we do not consider this the best of all possible outcomes, it is the one we are contending with right now, and it is no accident.

Appendix A

The Japanese Abacus

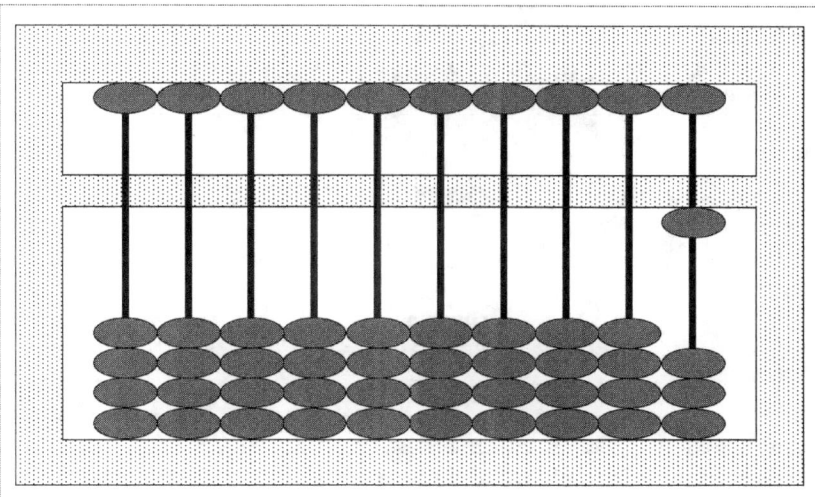

Diagram A-1
Base Ten Total = 1

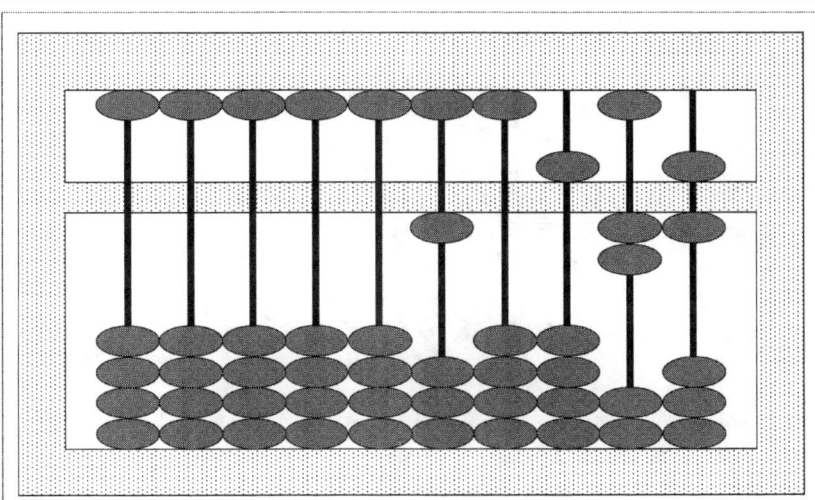

Diagram A-2
Base Ten Total = 10,526

Appendix B

A Binary Abacus

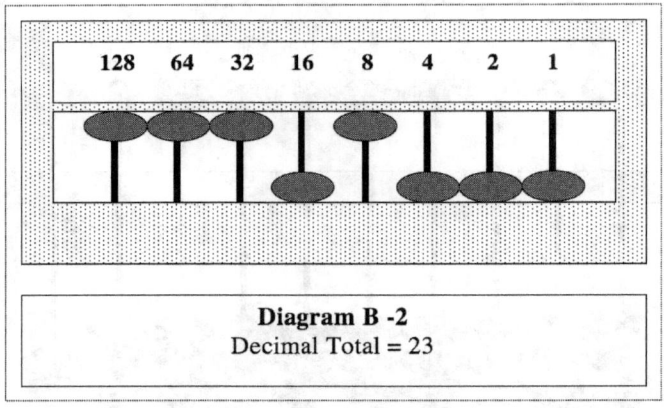

Diagram B -2
Decimal Total = 23

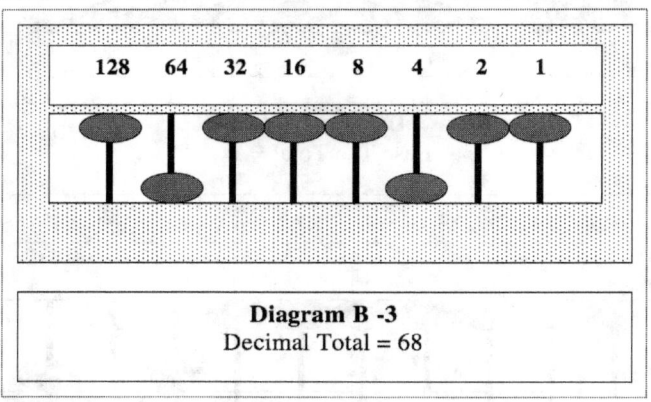

Diagram B -3
Decimal Total = 68

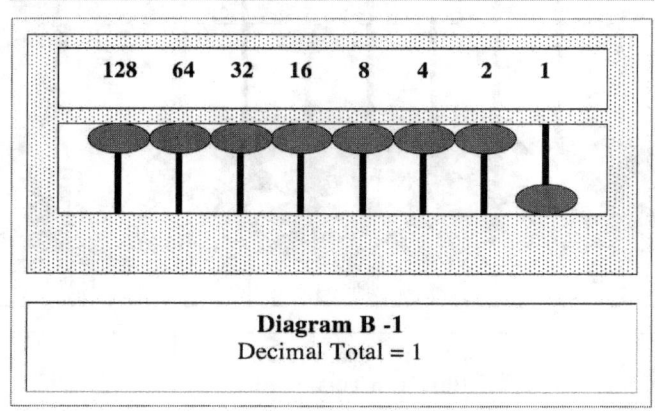

Diagram B -1
Decimal Total = 1

Appendix C

A Basic Relay Control Switch

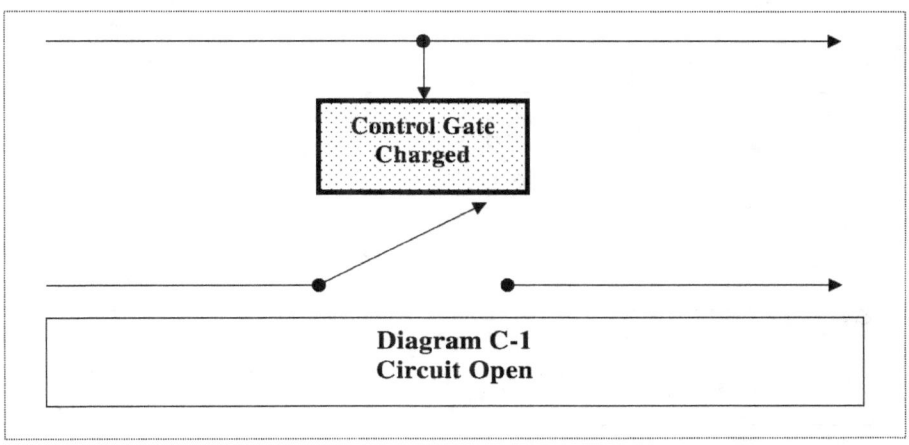

Diagram C-1
Circuit Open

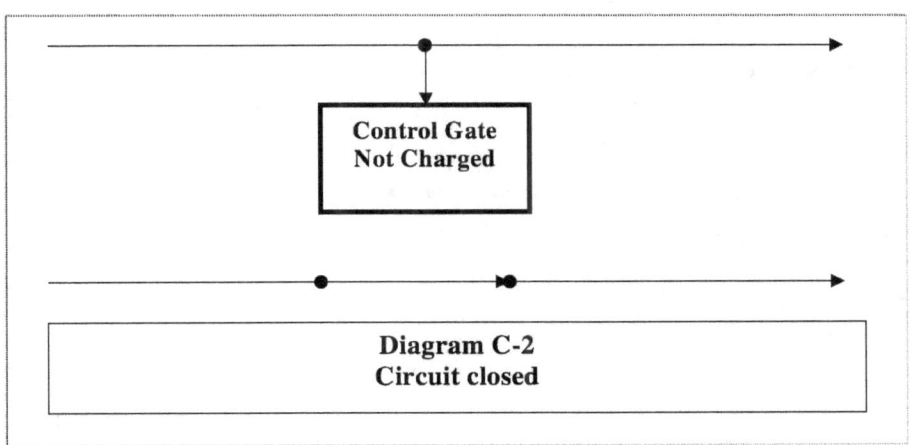

Diagram C-2
Circuit closed

Appendix D

Name	Diagram of Circuit	Truth Table			Equation	Explanation
AND		x_1	x_2	z	$z = x_1 x_2$	The gate will be closed (output a charge) only when a signal is present in both inputs.
		0	0	0		
		0	1	0		
		1	0	0		
		1	1	1		
OR		x_1	x_2	z	$z = x_1 + x_2$	The gate will be closed if either one or both inputs receive current.
		0	0	0		
		0	1	1		
		1	0	1		
		1	1	1		
NOT		x		z	$z = /x$	Any signal input opens the gate.
		0		1		
		1		0		
NAND		x_1	x_2	z	$z = /x_1 x_2$	The gate is closed unless there is signal in both inputs.
		0	0	1		
		0	1	1		
		1	0	1		
		1	1	0		
NOR		x_1	x_2	z	$z = /x_1 x_2$	The gate is closed unless it receives any configuration of input.
		0	0	1		
		0	1	0		
		1	0	0		
		1	1	0		
EXCLUSIVE-OR		x_1	x_2	z	$z = x_1 \oplus x_2$	The gate closes only when it receives signal from either input, but not both.
		0	0	0		
		0	1	1		
		1	0	1		
		1	1	0		

Figure D-1
Logic gates with explanations
(Adapted with modifications from Hayes 1988, 95)

Appendix E

A 'Half-adder' Addition Circuit

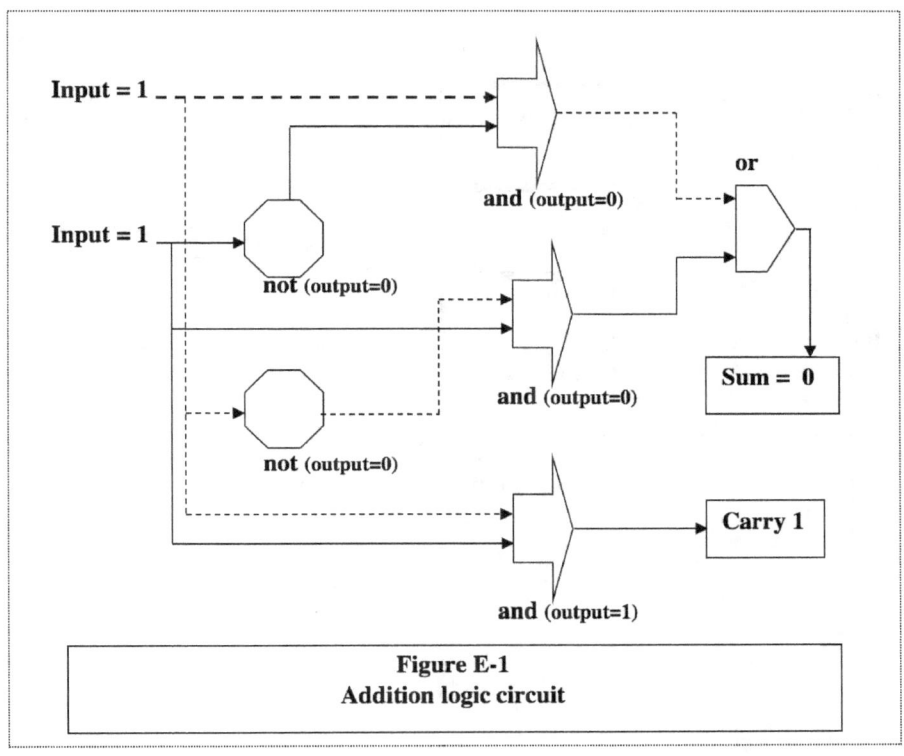

Figure E-1
Addition logic circuit

Appendix F

A 'Full-adder' Addition Circuit

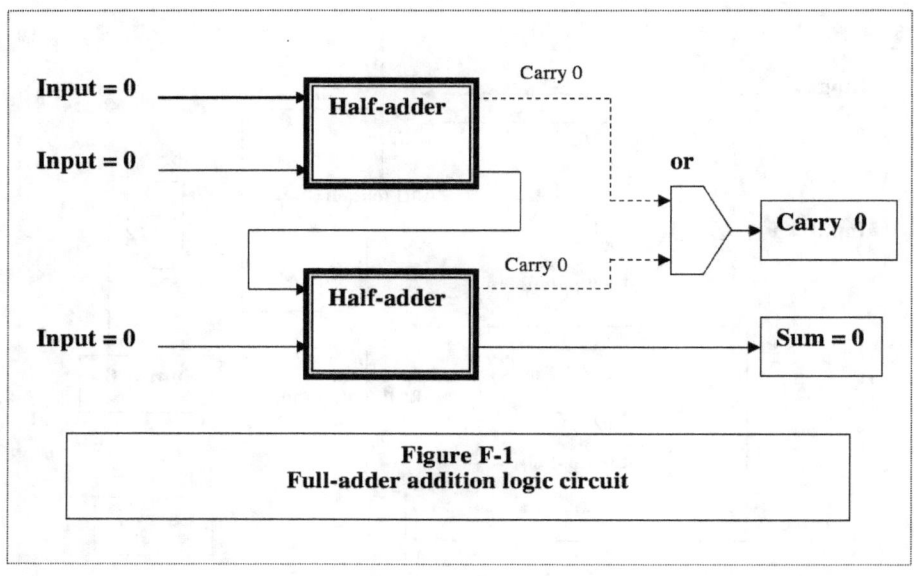

Figure F-1
Full-adder addition logic circuit

Works Cited

Baldwin, Thomas F., D. Stevens McVoy and Charles Steinfield. Convergence: Integrating Media, Information and Communication. London: Sage, 1996.

Barthes, Roland. Image, Music, Text. Stephen Heath (trans). New York: Noonday Press, 1988.

Benjamin, Walter. Illuminations. Hannah Arendt (ed.). Harry Zohn (trans). New York: Schocken Books, 1969.

Boole, George. An Investigation of the Laws of Thought, On Which Are Founded the Mathematical Theories of Logic and Probabilities. New York: Dover Publications, 1958.

Bush, Vannevar. "As We May Think." The Atlantic Monthly. 27 Feb. 2002 <http://www.ps.uni-sb.de/~duchier/pub/vbush/vbush.txt>. Originally published July 1945.

Calderbank, Robert and Neil Sloane. "Claude Shannon 1916-2001." Nature. 12 April 2001, v410, n6830: p.768.

Campbell-Kelly, Martin, and William Aspray. Computer: A History of the Information Machine. New York: BasicBooks, 1996.

Carey, James. Communication as Culture: Essays on Media and Society. Boston: Unwin/Hyman, 1989.

Carr, Herbert. The Monadology of Leibniz. London: Favil Press, 1930.

Chesher, Chris. "Why the Digital Computer is Dead". CTheory.net. 16 April 2002 <http://www.ctheory.net/text_file.asp?pick=334>.

Davis, Martin. Engines of Logic: Mathematicians and the Origin of the Computer. New York: W. W. Norton and Co. Ltd., 2000.

Dodge, Martin, and R. Kitchin. Mapping Cyberspace. London: Routledge, 2001.

Dreyfus, Hubert. What Computers Still Can't Do: A Critique of Artificial Reason. Cambridge: MIT Press, 1994.

Feenberg, Andrew. "Escaping the Iron Cage, or, Subversive Rationalization and Democratic Theory." Democratising Technology: Ethics, Risk, and Public Debate. Tilburg: International Centre for Human and Public Affairs, 1998. Online version: 8 Mar 2002 <http://www-rohan.sdsu.edu/faculty/feenberg/schom1.htm>.

Fisher, Dana R. and Larry Michael Wright. "On Utopias and Dystopias: Toward an Understanding of the Discourse

Surrounding the Internet." Journal of Computer Mediated
Communication. JCMC 6 (2), January 2001;
<http://www.ascusc.org/jcmc/vol6/issue2/fisher.html>.

Goldstine, Herman. The Computer: From Pascal to von
Neumann. New Jersey: Princeton University Press, 1993.

Hayes, John. Computer Architecture and Organization.
Toronto: McGraw-Hill Inc., 1988.

Horkheimer, Max, and Theodor Adorno. Dialectic of
Enlightenment. John Cumming (Trans). New York:
Continuum Publishing Co., 1995.

Howe, Denis (ed.). The Free Online Dictionary of Computing.
13 April 2002
<http://burks.brighton.ac.uk/burks/foldoc/27/28.htm>.
Originally published 30 April 1999.

Innis, Harold. Empire & Communications. David Godfrey (ed).
Victoria: Press Porcépic Ltd., 1986.

Innis, Harold. The Bias of Communication. Toronto:
University of Toronto Press, 1991.

Kittler, Friedrich. "There is No Software." CTheory .net. 16
April 2002 <http://www.ctheory.net/text_file.asp?pick=74>.
Originally published 18 Oct. 1995.

Latour, Bruno. "Where are the Missing Masses? The Sociology
of a Few Mundane Artifacts." Shaping Technology/Building
Society: Studies in Sociotechnical Change. Weibe Bijker and
John Law (eds). Cambridge Mass: MIT Press, 1992.

Lyotard, Jean-Francois. "The Post-Modern Condition: A Report on Knowledge." Readings in Social Theory: The Classic Tradition to Post-Modernism. James Farganis (ed.). Toronto: McGraw-Hill, 1993.

Manovich, Lev. "From the Externalization of the Psyche to the Implantation of Technology." Mind Revolution: Interface Brain/Computer. Florian Rotzer (ed.). Munchen: Akademie Zum Dritten Juhrtausond, 1995.

Manovich, Lev. The Language of New Media. Cambridge: MIT Press, 2002.

Massumi, Brian. "Realer Than Real: The Simulacrum According to Deleuze and Guattari". 27 Feb. 2002 <http://www.anuy.edu.au/HRC/first_and_last/works/realer.htm>. Originally published in Copyright. 1, 1987.

McLuhan, Marshall. "Media and Cultural Change," in The Essential McLuhan. Anansi, 1995.

McLuhan, Marshall.   Understanding Media. Mentor/Penguin, 1964.

Munster, Anna. "Digitality: Approximate Aesthetics." CTheory .net. 16 April 2002 <http://www.ctheory.net/printer.asp?id=290>. Originally published 2001.

Postman, Neil. Technopoly: The Surrender of Culture to Technology. Toronto: Random House of Canada Ltd., 1993.

Redshaw, Kerry. "Claude Shannon (1916-2001)". Pioneers. 2 May 2002 <http://www.kerryr.net/poineers/shannon.htm>. Originally published 2001.

Rockeby, David. "Transforming Mirrors: Subjectivity and Control in Interactive Media". Critical Issues in Electronic Media. Simon Penny (ed.). New York: State University of New York Press, 1995.

Rodowick, D. N. Reading the Figural or, Philosophy After the New Media. Durham: Duke University Press.

Ross, George. "Leibniz: The Monadology Running Commentary." 5 June 2002 <http://www.prs-ltsn.ac.uk/generic/screentexts/monexpl.html>. Copyright 1999.

Selvia, John. "A Binary Primer: Introduction." 12 Feb. 2002 <http://www.dnaco.net/~ivanjs/binprime.html>. Copyright 1995.

Sems, Marty. "It's Just Common Sense." Smart Computing. July 2002, v13, n7: p. 7.

Shannon, Claude and Warren Weaver. The Mathematical Theory of Communication. Chicago: University of Illinois Press, 1978.

The Radical Academy. "The Origin of Ideas: A Critique of Some Philosophical Positions." Philosophical Critiques. 5 June 2002 <http://radicalacademy.com/adiphilcritideas.htm#leibniz>. Copyright 2001.

Von Neumann, John. First Draft of a Report on the EDVAC. Michael Godfrey (ed.). Stanford: Electrical Engineering Department, Stanford University, 1992.

Wood, Gaby. Living Dolls: A Magical History of the Quest For Mechanical Life. London: Faber and Faber Ltd., 2002.